People and Tourism

People and Tourism

Issues and Attitudes In the Jamaican Hospitality Industry

Hopeton S. Dunn

and

Leith L. Dunn

---

with contributions by
James Samuels
and
Chandana Jayawardena

A r a w a k publications
17 Kensington Crescent
Kingston 5

ISBN 976 8189 03 7

06 05 04 03 02 01   5 4 3 2 1

NATIONAL LIBRARY OF JAMAICA
CATALOGUING IN PUBLICATION DATA

Dunn, Hopeton S.
People and tourism : issues and attitudes in the Jamaican hospitality
industry / by Hopeton S. Dunn and Leith L. Dunn; with contributions
by James Samuels, Chandana Jayawardena.
p. ;   cm.
Includes bibliographical references

ISBN 976-8189-03-7

1.Tourist trade - Jamaica - Surveys
I.   Dunn, Leith L.   II. Title

338.47917292 - dc. 20

Credits:
Photos
Cover; p. 109 – © Robert Armstrong 2001. "Workers in the Lumber Yard".
Acrylic on canvas
Pages xv, 3, 10, 24, 43, 55, 67, 80, 92, 109, 122, 129, 136, 147– made available
for use by kind courtesy of the Jamaica Tourist Board

Illustration
p. 80 – Cartoon by Las May. Courtesy of the *Daily Gleaner*

Set in Plantin Light 10/13 x 24
Cover and book design by Robert Harris
Printed in the United States of America

Contents

Introduction
Integrating People and Tourism
the Prospects and Challenges
(James Samuels) / *xv*

Section I
Talking Tourism: Mapping Jamaican Attitudes
Report of a National Research Study / *1*

Section 2
Visitor Harassment in Negril, Jamaica
A Community Case Study / 65

In Retrospect
Community Tourism
Applying the Lessons in the Caribbean
(Chandana Jayawardena) / 147

List of Figures

List of Tables

Foreword

Adrian Robinson
Chairman, Jamaica Tourist Board

I have always been of the view that in order to succeed, tourism in Jamaica requires the permission of the people. Tourism's future, and its ability as a major economic activity to contribute to our country's growth, will largely be determined by the perceptions, understandings and attitudes of our people, and their responses to the pertinent issues of both participation in, and beneficial involvement with, the industry.

Professional, scientific research has always formed the basis for planning the work of the Jamaica Tourist Board, both in marketing the JAMAICA destination brand overseas and in forging local partnerships.

This study, which combines quantitative and qualitative research methods, including community meetings and panel discussions, has therefore been of immense value to the Board's work.

One of the original studies "Jamaican Attitudes to Tourism" was produced for the JTB by Dr Hopeton Dunn and Dr Leith Dunn and forms part of our on-going effort to learn more about public attitudes and perceptions of the industry. The knowledge gained from this study has guided our work to promote fuller public understanding of their role in tourism development and to broaden the range of people's participation. The second study is no less valuable a contribution to understanding issues affecting the growth of the industry in areas such as Negril.

The findings of the studies published here show that although the overwhelming majority of Jamaicans recognize the value of tourism, there are residual negative views in some cases. They also raise questions and concerns as to how or whether the industry benefited persons individually.

The JTB has already responded and continues to respond to the lessons from the research.

In the areas of education and community involvement, an intensive public education programme embraces a range of projects in schools, the most important of which is the Infusion Programme. The term 'infusion' is used because it has the objective of integrating tourism concepts into the existing school curriculum at all levels: early childhood, primary and secondary through to grade nine. Schools throughout Jamaica will be participating in this programme by the end of 2001.

At the community level, new local festivals such as the St Elizabeth Shrimp and Craft Festival, the Portland Jerk Festival, and the Old Harbour Bay Fish and Bammy Festival are celebrations of both the natural and cultural environments of local communities. Members of the community who would not normally have seen themselves as being directly involved in tourism, now participate in planning and staging these events and share in the economic benefits. Such events are being encouraged and supported by the JTB in recognition of the fact that the sustainability and growth of tourism as a national enterprise require the acceptance, support and involvement of the Jamaican people.

The Jamaica Tourist Board sees the publication of this book as an excellent way of sharing the knowledge we have gained with all Jamaicans and, in particular, our industry partners. For Jamaica to reap greater benefits from tourism, we must work together and if we are to work together effectively, the knowledge we have should also be shared.

We are sure that you will find the information in this publication both instructive and educational.

Preface and Acknowledgments

This publication embodies two major research studies conducted in Jamaica on popular attitudes to tourism, people's perceptions of tourism messages and their attitudes to harassment in the hospitality industry.

The first research report presented here is a national survey conducted among 1,025 respondents in all fourteen parishes. It includes detailed reports of nine focus group discussions and three major town meetings throughout the country. The preliminary findings of this islandwide survey have served as a central policy-making tool for Jamaican tourism planners and have been in demand by Caribbean hoteliers, researchers and students of tourism management since its completion in late 1999. This publication represents the first public release of the updated study, reflecting the quantitative findings, in-depth qualitative profiles and the analyses which have already influenced policy approaches at the highest levels of the industry.

The second study presents the results of research conducted in the resort town of Negril on the causes, incidence and consequences of harassment of visitors. We document the views of residents, workers in the industry, managers, persons convicted of harassment and the views of tourists themselves who were on vacation in Negril. This study, initially done in 1994, was updated in March and April 2001 by additional field research. Findings of the surveys and in-depth interviews with hotel managers, sex workers, craft vendors, 'informal tour guides' and so-called harassers in the resort community are presented. This community case study of Negril provides relevant baseline data on an issue never before explored in this detail in the Caribbean.

The initial version of the National Tourism Attitude Survey was commissioned by the Jamaica Tourist Board and is published here in a revised and updated version as Section 1. The Negril Study on Visitor Harassment which was commissioned by the JTB, Tourism Action Plan Ltd (TAP) and the Negril Resort Board is also revised and with additional fieldwork data, is presented in Section 2. We thank these organizations for providing the opportunity to conduct the initial research. We are grateful to the chairman of the JTB, Mr Adrian Robinson, who provided active encouragement and contributed the Foreword to this volume. We also gratefully acknowledge the support of Director of Tourism Mrs Fay Pickersgill and the assistance provided by members of her management team and technical staff, past and present. In particular, we thank Mr Sam McCook, Mr Trevor Riley, Mr Roy Miller, Ms Essie Gardner, Mr Tony Lowrie and members of the administrative staff. From the side of the Negril Study, both Mrs Stephanie Belcher and Mrs Carolyn Hayle formerly of TAP, provided invaluable assistance, as did Mr Greg Keesling former Chairman of the Negril Resort Board and other members of the Negril tourism community. Inspector Colley, of the Negril Police Station was also of invaluable assistance in our efforts to research the issue of crime and visitor harassment in the area. We thank Mr James Samuels, hotelier and former President of the Jamaica Hotel and Tourist Association (JHTA), who warmly welcomed the data and analysis provided in the Attitude Study. He also kindly agreed to write the introduction to this published edition. In addition, we thank Dr Chandana Jayawardena, Senior Lecturer and Academic Director of the MSc Programme in Tourism and Hospitality Management at the University of the West Indies (UWI), Mona for contributing the retrospective analysis at the end of this volume. Thanks also to the many other stakeholders who supported the research process, including the Ministry of Tourism, and the UWI. We are also grateful for the technical support of Mrs Kristin Fox, Ms Laurianne Brown, Dr Paul Martin and to members of the fieldwork interviewing teams, primarily made up of former CARIMAC Research Methods students.

We acknowledge in particular the hundreds of Jamaicans and civil society groups who willingly shared their views and made a valuable contribution to our understanding of citizens' perceptions and concerns about the industry. Their openness and willingness to share their opinions highlight the importance of popular dialogue and consultation for the future development of the industry and the country.

Finally, our special thanks to Jessica and Jamani Dunn for their assistance and understanding and to the many other members of our family for their consistent support.

Hopeton S. Dunn and Leith L. Dunn

Abbreviations

AWOJA	Association of Women's Organizations of Jamaica
AWU	Antigua Workers' Union
AYF	Area Youth Foundation
BPCA	Bluefields People's Community Association
CTO	Caribbean Tourism Organization
CHA	Caribbean Hotel Association
GATS	General Agreement on Trade in Services
GDP	gross domestic product
HEART Trust/ NTA	Human Employment and Resource Training Trust/ National Training Agency
IDB	Inter-Americian Development Bank
ILO	International Labour Organization
IVA	Itinerant Vendors Association
JACS	Jamaica Amalgamated Cable Systems Limited
JHTA	Jamaica Hotel and Tourist Association
JIS	Jamaica Information Service
JTB	Jamaica Tourist Board
KMRB	Kingston Metropolitan Resort Board
NGO	non-governmental organization
NJDP	Northern Jamaica Development Project
OPM	Office of the Prime Minister
ORCVA	Ocho Rios Craft Vendors Association
PIOJ	Planning Institute of Jamaica
PJCA	Portmore Joint Citizens Association
PRIDE	Programme for the Resettlement and Integrated Development Enterprises
RTFT	Report on the Task Force of Tourism
SET	Sustaining the Environment and Tourism
STATIN	Statistical Institute of Jamaica
TAP	Tourism Action Plan Limited
TIE	Theatre in Education
TPDCo	Tourism Product Development Company
UDC	Urban Development Corporation
UWI	The University of the West Indies

Integrating People and Tourism

The Prospects and Challenges

JAMES SAMUELS*

Within the Caribbean, tourism is our biggest earner, accounting for a third of total output and a quarter of all jobs. Over 45 percent of export earnings and more than 75 percent of foreign investments regionally were derived from tourism in the year 2000 and visitors to the Caribbean spent an estimated US$17.773 billion. The World Tourism Organization continues to project growth in the industry. When one looks closely at these growth trends, it is easy to understand why almost every country is involved in tourism and why for some, it is the single most important economic sector.

The value of world tourism arrivals at the start of the new century was estimated at US$476 billion excluding airfares. Tourism drives major social and economic opportunities because at its best, it positively affects life in the entire community. The universal growth of tourism as a major economic activity resides partly in the global realization that the essential ingredients

*James Samuels is a Jamaican hotelier and former president of the Jamaica Hotel and Tourist Association.

required for its success are already in abundance within host countries. The physical layout of a country as well as its social norms of foods, music, environment, history, people and culture remain the basic raw materials for entering the tourism industry. Within this mix of ingredients, the component referred to as people remains the single most important variable. It is people who add texture and meaning to the overall recreational experience of visitors.

As Caribbean countries seek to foster growth in tourism, research and analysis will be needed to provide insight into the attitudes and behavioural realities with which we are confronted. This book is a major contribution to that process and represents the kind of research and analysis needed to deepen our understanding of how to fashion a sustainable tourism product.

At every level, tourism has the capacity to be heavily integrated into the total economy. For example, the transportation sector can be integrated through car rental companies, tour companies, taxis and airlines with both scheduled flights and charters. Greater integration between agriculture and tourism can have a direct impact on a host of agro-industries that offer benefits to the local farmer. The accommodation sector with its variety of products presents a potpourri of opportunities for small and large investors as well as communities. Whether the business relates to a villa or an apartment, a small hotel, an attraction or craft shop, the tourism industry offers all sectors of a society the opportunity, not readily seen in other sectors, to participate at both the economic and social level. It is this wide-ranging potential for economic integration that fuels global participation, acceptance and success of the industry. The city of Orlando in Florida, for example, would hardly be the same without the integrating tourism component named 'Disney'.

At the other end of the spectrum, tourism that is not properly managed can produce enormous social and environmental problems. One factor that can trigger such problems is land. Invariably tourism development leads to a rapid change in the price of land, thus affecting the ability of individuals in host communities to own a home. At another level, the quality of the environment can represent the difference between success and failure in the industry.

Tourism and globalization

Globalization is driving the tourism industry. As a service sector, tourism falls within the ambit of the General Agreement on Trade in Services (GATS), administered under the World Trade Organization (WTO). In responding to the global challenges, some companies within the industry have undergone re-structuring and have emerged as part of the new sunshine economy, employing sensitive human relations policies and the best available technologies. Other companies associated with the 'older economy' must now re-engineer their processes and become more productive if they are going to successfully compete. In operating within this culture of 'the new economy', all industry participants must devote special attention to the twin imperatives of people and technology. Inevitably, managing the people component and the social infrastructure is already developing as the key challenge within and outside of resort communities.

People and tourism

As highlighted in this study, the attitudes of people are important in determining the level of success the industry enjoys. People's attitudes are the platform from which we deliver quality service and interactions with visitors. If people are not in tune with the industry at all levels, from the street cleaner to the large hotel owner, the consequences will be disastrous for our economy. We must therefore seek to be as informed as we can be about our host populations, their views and attitudes. At the same time, we must also create mechanisms that will allow the industry to keep our people informed about the sector.

Valuing tourism research

Jamaica and the wider Caribbean are fortunate to have both the University of the West Indies (UWI) and the University of Technology providing research and training as well as bringing intellectual rigour to many of the complex issues confronting the hospitality industry. To its credit, the UWI recently produced a specially annotated bibliography of works in progress or already completed on tourism in the Caribbean (Cassell et al. 2000). Among the works that stood out in that UWI bibliography were the two research studies by Hopeton Dunn and Leith Dunn which form the subject matter for this book. The contents are compulsory reading for all Caribbean tourism professionals and moreso for our decision-makers. The value of their research in assisting our efforts toward internal reform and sustainable development cannot be underestimated.

The value and impact of tourism should go beyond the established resort communities. As the authors clearly indicate, the solutions to issues must be sought in a national framework of responsibility and nurturing of the industry. In agreeing with this approach, I further suggest that planning for the future should take place against the background of an understanding of the historical context of the industry. While it is true that the history of tourism throughout the region is one that emanates from the actions of a privileged elite, workers, governments and the people have indispensably aided the sector's development at large.

One of the realities of tourism in the Caribbean is that it was born at a time when economic power was still the prerogative of the landed gentry and when the vast majority of the population remained grossly disenfranchised. In Jamaica, the United Fruit Company had a very significant role in the introduction of tourism, having been part of the Port Antonio banana export experience. In the closing decade of the nineteenth century, a businessman, Lorenzo Baker, who was involved in shipping bananas from the north coast of Jamaica to the eastern seaboard of the United States, hit on the idea of filling his empty southbound ships with American tourists, giving them five days at sea followed by a hotel holiday in Port Antonio. He later constructed his own hotel, The Titchfield, which grew to 150 rooms, an enormous capacity for the 1890s.

Despite these early beginnings, the industry only began to take shape in the 1950s with the Abe Issa family in the east and the Delissers in the west creating mainly winter holidays for American visitors. In those days, the winter season began with great fanfare, and perhaps the fact that it was the only season contributed to a broad-based preparation. Hotel owners would seek to completely refurbish their properties and the resort towns would make sure they were painted and ready for the start of each season on December 15. Notwithstanding good hotel rates and high occupancy levels, very few of these hotels ever opened after April 15 of the following year. The business was a highly seasonal one and great effort was made, not just by the few hoteliers but also by people in the wider host communities, to make the visitors welcome.

It is also of interest to note that the current resort towns were then little coastal villages. Only Montego Bay in western Jamaica could have been called a town. As such, we did not really have an industry. Very significantly, Jamaicans who worked in tourism mainly occupied line staff positions. The

Jamaican middle class had very little to do with the industry, many equating the various jobs with that of the house slaves. There was little meaningful interaction between the visitors and the Jamaican people at large. The process reinforced the syndrome of 'them' and 'us'. The fact is, this was a business that was not integrated within the Jamaican economy and enjoyed negative perceptions among sections of the population. Arguably, this may well mirror the rest of the Caribbean during this period.

Over the years since then, the industry has grown extensively, and far more people have benefited from its expansion. However, many of the social issues present at the time of its origin have remained within the industry in the period since political independence. The tendency for industry benefits to accrue mainly to a dominant elite, the concentration of visitors in certain 'tourist areas', the stark disparity between social conditions in those resort areas and life in the adjoining local communities all remain as important challenges highlighted by this study.

Creating local stakeholders

The need for faster national economic growth no doubt dictated the political decision to expand the industry. The role of the Urban Development Corporation (UDC) in facilitating or constructing critical infrastructure, starting in the late sixties and early seventies, was crucial. The UDC spearheaded the construction of hotels such as the Holiday Inn, Wyndham Rosehall, Trelawny Beach, the entire Ocho Rios harbour and many other developments. In the corporate area, Hilton Kingston Hotel, the present Courtleigh Hotel, the Le Meridien Jamaica Pegasus and the now closed Ocean and Forum hotels also fall within this period of major development.

The seventies saw the emergence of a fully developed industry, offering year round services in most of the resorts. This was also the age of the mass traveller. With the construction of new high-rise properties and brand names such as Intercontinental, Hyatt, Holiday Inn and Hilton International, Jamaica seemed ready to take advantage of the international investment flows in tourism. Unfortunately, the expectations for the industry could not be met. Notwithstanding the major investment by the public sector and global investors, the people of Jamaica were not actively brought on board and so remained ambivalent toward the industry.

Limited transitions

By the mid seventies, our ambitions for a vibrant industry lay in tatters. The major international brands whose coat tails we had hoped to ride on were leaving Jamaica. The Government of Jamaica which guaranteed the financing of these hotels was faced with the prospect of closing them whilst still having to service their debts or operate them as going concerns. This is where the policy of having Jamaicans as understudies began to bear fruit. The government, as major equity owner, insisted that each hotel had to provide training and an understudy programme for Jamaicans to learn about the operation and management of the industry. This policy had far-reaching implications that went on to permanently shape and influence the tourism landscape. Not least among these were fundamental shifts in both the ownership and operation of hotels.

As some key players among the international chains left, a new state agency, National Hotels and Properties came into its own with a strong policy towards infusion of Jamaican professionals in the sector. Whilst the majority of Jamaican nationals had limited experience as owners and managers, the corps of Jamaican professionals which was in training rose to the challenge and helped to keep the industry going. Although the involvement of these and other Jamaican professionals within the industry deepened, the wider public remained distant, particularly in the urban capital. This situation was not lost on the government of the day. The response took the form of new strategies, including the establishment of the Jamaica Tourist Board's Discover Jamaica and Vacation Sales programmes, with the specific mandate to sell Jamaica to Jamaicans.

This represented a fundamental shift in policy by government to aggressively encourage Jamaicans to both discover Jamaica and to vacation at home. The civil servant who enjoyed 'home leave' and saw this as a trip to England, was encouraged to spend his or her vacation in Jamaican hotels. Companies and other commercial business were given tax exemptions from the cost of vacation packages as incentives for their staff. This facility still exists today. The interim results were quite dramatic. In 1976, Jamaicans registered approximately 9,000 person visits to hotels in Jamaica. By the end of 1977, the number of person visits had jumped to 129,000 with the concomitant economic spin-off to big and small hotels alike. However, the most significant result came from the fact that Jamaicans had now begun the process of participation. Thus began the challenge of creating a significant shift in Jamaican attitudes toward tourism.

At the same time, the Jamaicans who heeded the call to vacation at home were to experience their own set of horror stories. The hotels also had their hands full in dealing with the needs and attitudes of the domestic market. As this study indicates, prevailing negative treatment of locals in some resort hotels is but a continuing reflection of that hoped-for adjustment, which has not been made at the level of many hotel properties, their managers and employees to this day.

Emergence of all-inclusives

During all this, other more positive events were continuing to shape the contemporary industry. We now began to experience the emergence of a significant Jamaican private sector in the industry. It was in 1976 that we saw what was to become one of the most revolutionary products in the development of tourism, worldwide. Negril Beach Village was opened by Frank Rance (now FDR Holidays) under John Issa's new chain. The design concept was new and so was the village. Once you paid the designated daily rate, the village not only gave you a room, but you had tennis, squash, shuffle board, a host of water-sports, 24 hours of food service, 24 hours bar service and entertainment every night. Even cigarettes were thrown in. The product was and remains a success today. SuperClubs, as the chain came to be known, is now a major international brand.

A few years later, another Jamaican entrepreneur took the leap of faith in yet another derivative of that successful all-inclusive experiment. This time we had a luxury product with just about every imaginable ingredient offered for couples only. Gordon 'Butch' Stewart is now a Jamaican icon, respected worldwide for his Sandals brand. However, the all-inclusive product was not without its social and economic implications, locally – an issue which again receives specific attention in this book.

Today the Jamaican tourism industry is over 80 percent Jamaican owned. With Sandals and SuperClubs as world leaders, we also have several smaller chains and individual owners. We have villa colonies and luxury hotels. The industry spawns successive cohorts of highly respected professionals, and to the great majority of visitors from overseas the quality of the Jamaican product is surpassed only by its variety. The spread of investment in the industry by Jamaicans from every socioeconomic stratum is widening. Pension fund managers have invested significant sums. Nevertheless, to the majority of ordinary Jamaicans, there are major cracks in this burnished facade.

Transforming the negatives

We still have a long way to go, notwithstanding the gains. This study, originally commissioned by the Jamaica Tourist Board, points to several issues which will need to be addressed more urgently. These include issues such as crime, economic disparity and problems of poor infrastructure. These and other concerns have been in existence for a long time. Harassment remains a core problem. There are, at the same time, many overwhelming positives. Among these are the level of foreign exchange earnings, jobs in both primary and secondary industries and the number of people now displaying positive attitudes towards tourism, all of which augur well for the future of the industry.

For me, one of the important issues raised in the research is that there is still a significant disjuncture between the wider population and the leading beneficiaries of the industry. Notwithstanding the importance with which people now view tourism, its future can only be guaranteed if this disparity is successfully addressed. This situation also applies to the employees in the industry. I am reminded in the study, for example, that we have failed to address effectively the accommodation needs of workers as essential players in the industry. It would also appear that tourism development has consistently failed to successfully address the needs of the residents of new communities that are the resorts and even the wider communities, which would provide strategic support, like our farmers and artisans and performing artistes.

An important contribution made by this book is the critical evaluation it makes of certain messages contained in our promotion of tourism. It is clear that in developing and executing domestic marketing programmes, certain critical components of the messages will need to be included, such as the protection of the environment and the abandonment of some stereotypical, old-fashioned images of our people.

The fact that the majority of our people view the management of the industry positively and regard the industry as important is an indication of a supportive social environment. In addition, the perception that most Jamaicans (54.3 percent) view tourists as ordinary people, would also suggest that there are strong opportunities for shared experiences. But there are also signs of dire consequences if the opportunity to effect positive changes in people is not grasped. People's involvement in the industry through a more integrated/holistic approach to product delivery remains a central need.

The future

As we advance into this new century, research about the new customer is also emerging. We are discovering that recreational travellers are interested not just in hotels, but more so in the broad experience provided by entire communities. It therefore becomes critical that the primary components of the experience, the people and their lifestyles are recognized as such and programmes implemented to empower and involve people in all practical ways.

The JTB's strong emphasis on local festivals is an emerging strategy that seeks to involve the broader community in the tourism experience. Events marketing which is being hailed as the most powerful catalyst in attracting large international participation is also being strongly encouraged through food, pastimes as well as music festivals. Although we have always intuitively seen this kind of activity as smart, the research findings have provided concrete sociological evidence that focusing on our people provides the surest way for success.

I challenge and encourage my colleagues both in Jamaica and the wider Caribbean to read and act upon the contents of this important publication. Its analysis is consistent with the current strategy of the Caribbean Hotel Association aimed at having the benefits of tourism distributed more equitably among all sectors and cascade more visibly to the people at large. These findings represent a part of a critical road map that we cannot afford to ignore as we seek to strengthen and expand our tourism industries.

SECTION I

Talking Tourism
Mapping Jamaican Attitudes

Report of a National Research Study

CHAPTER 1

Framing The Research

Trends in Tourism Development

According to the World Tourism Organization, by the year 2000 the industry accounted for 10.5 percent of all international consumer expenditures, 11.8 percent of capital investment and 6.8 percent of all government spending. It provided direct and indirect employment for an estimated 231 million people worldwide and contributed an estimated US$800 billion in personal and corporate taxes in 1998.

The industry is growing at a steady pace globally. International tourist arrivals grew by 7 percent per annum between 1950 and 1997, and are expected to grow by between 4 percent and 5 percent per annum for the next decade.

The wider Caribbean is regarded as one of the most tourism dependent regions of the world, accounting for one in four jobs and close to a quarter of the gross domestic product (GDP). The hospitality industry is the region's largest earner of legitimate hard currency, from the estimated 12 million stopover visitors and 9 million cruise passengers a year. The Caribbean is also the most popular cruise destination globally, with more than 42 percent of liners sailing the region. The nearest competitor, Europe, accounts for just 20 percent of global cruises. As a parallel to dominance in the cruise segment, the rate of growth of regional stopover visitors increased by 4 percent in 1999. While this is twice the rate of growth of the Jamaican industry between 1998 and 1999, it is a fraction of the growth rate of the biggest performers of the region. Cuba continues to be the fastest growing Caribbean destination, with growth in stopover visitors exceeding 17 percent between 1998 and 1999. The Dominican Republic registered 14 percent growth rate, with the other double-digit performer in 1999 being the US Virgin Islands (10 percent).

By the end of the twentieth century Jamaica's tourism industry hosted over 1.32 million stopover visitors and a further 907,000 cruise ship passengers annually. The industry is the fastest growing sector in the economy and continues to be the major source of foreign exchange earning. In the baseline year 2000, net foreign exchange contribution to the economy was US $800 million and total visitor expenditure was in the region of US $1.362 million. Tourism's contribution to Jamaica's GDP was estimated by the Ministry of Tourism to be 8 percent, and employment (direct and indirect) in the sector was recorded at 75,000 Jamaicans.

Government has set a ten-year growth plan in place, time-tabled between the 2000 baseline and the year 2010. According to the Master Plan targets, it is expected that stopover arrivals will grow annually by 5.5 percent to 2.2 million land-based visitors by 2010. The plan anticipates that cruise passengers will increase by 10 percent a year to equal stopover visitors at 2.2 million tourists in the same ten-year period. Foreign exchange earning is expected to triple in the next decade and contribution to GDP to increase from 8 percent to 15 percent. The plan projects that by 2010 some 130,000 Jamaicans will be employed in the industry.

Clearly, these are great expectations for an industry viewed as having major development potential. Not only is it the 'cash crop' of the Jamaican economy, but it is also the major income earner in the Caribbean and one of the fastest growing industries globally.

Despite the optimistic forecasts and its record of significant overall contribution to the economy, the hospitality industry in Jamaica is very vulnerable and reflects both positive and negative trends. Over the five-year period 1995 to 2000, stopover arrivals averaged 1.3 million visitors and reflected only sluggish growth (see Table 1.1).

Table 1.1   Stopover Arrivals to Jamaica

Year	Stopovers
1995	1,147
1996	1,693
1997	1,192
1998	1,225
1999	1,248
2000	1,320

Source: Jamaica Tourist Board Statistics

As the regional tourism figures indicate, the Caribbean hospitality industry is becoming increasingly competitive. Each territory offers sun, sand and high quality in hotel accommodation. What will distinguish one destination from the other will be the creativity and special warmth of the people, and the quality and uniqueness of the entertainment, food and other cultural and environmental attractions.

In this competitive context, Jamaica cannot afford to be complacent and has a great deal of ground to cover. On the positive side, the number of cruise passengers and stopover visitors more than doubled during the past ten years and longer stopover visits increased by 40 percent in the same period. Importantly, as well, our study confirmed that the great majority of Jamaicans regard tourism as an important industry. However, a majority of people also hold the view that the industry is not structured to benefit a wide enough cross-section of the population. This is a concern dealt with extensively in the study with perspectives from a wide range of respondents.

The industry and the country are also facing other major challenges. The persistent problem of visitor harassment and an uncomfortable level of crime and violence nationally, are among these. Police reports indicate that in the three-year period 1996–1998, a total of 718 crimes directly affecting overseas visitors were reported, an average of close to 240 incidents a year. While these incidents are often relatively minor and represent a small proportion of the national figures, they remain a significant deterrent to achieving the targeted growth rates in the Master Plan. The frequency and detrimental effects of these and other forms of visitor harassment have been shown to limit the growth prospects and sustainability of the industry. (See study on visitor harassment in Negril in Part 2 of this volume; see also Stone 1989; Boxill 1995.)

Despite being located in a breathtakingly beautiful part of the world, despite being part of a regional and global industry experiencing sustained growth and with a forecast for even greater contributions to the national economy, Jamaican tourism continues to operate in unstable and unsustainable circumstances. Unless pressing issues of social inequality, employment and education within and outside of the industry are addressed, symptoms such as visitor harassment, petty crimes and occasional popular upheavals will continue to bedevil the sector regarded as Jamaica's main economic lifeline.

This chapter is about unveiling popular perceptions of these deeper problems and their more visible manifestations in the industry. We hope to contribute to a deeper and more intimate understanding the issues at stake and give voice to some perceived solutions. Among other things, this section discloses the need for fundamental reform of intra-industry relationships and for more creative and widespread public education about the benefits of tourism to the national economy.

Rationale

There is now a growing recognition that the industry cannot develop without the active support and positive involvement of the wider Jamaican population, both within and outside of resort communities. As part of this, there is also the need for a greater level of awareness and support for the industry among people in Jamaica and among Jamaicans living abroad. It was against this background that the initial study was commissioned by the Jamaica Tourist Board. The baseline data presented here are intended to contribute to further improving industry policy planning and to enhance the industry's local communication and outreach programmes. According to the 2001 draft of the Tourism Master Plan, government aims "to develop tourism in such a way that it meets the needs of today's residents and visitors, while protecting and improving the opportunities of future generations to meet these needs".

The five major objectives designed to achieve this are:

- growth based on a sustainable market position
- enhancement of the visitor experience

- community based development
- the building of an inclusive industry
- environmental sustainability

Effective implementation of these objectives requires the knowledge, co-operation and support of citizens from all strata as well as their on-going contribution to the policy-making process. The initial findings from this national research study have already contributed to and are reflected in the Master Plan and in the on-going policy planning at the level of the JTB. The updating and publication of the findings in book form will, we hope, enable a wider audience to share in and critically evaluate people's opinions from the community level as the Plan moves further into implementation.

Research objectives and methods

The aim was to identify popular Jamaican attitudes to tourism. The views and perceptions of different strata of the population about tourism were carefully and systematically documented in two phases. New qualitative research data gathered in March and April 2001 were used to update the islandwide study conducted between March and May 1999. There was a high correlation between the findings of 1999 and those in 2001.

The quantitative and qualitative data-gathering methods used included:

- A questionnaire survey administered to 1,025 persons in all parishes.
- Nine focus group discussion sessions, conducted with a wide cross-section of participants varying in age, location, sex and level of involvement with the industry.
- In-depth interviews with a range of informants and specialists in the industry.
- Participant observation of tourism related service delivery, meetings and events.
- Participatory research, involving a specially organized community meeting in Portmore, St Catherine. A panel discussion was transmitted live to cable television subscribers in the community and a cross-section of residents invited to present their views via telephone on tourism related issues.
- Documentary research, using a variety of sources (tourism reports, government statistical data, newspaper clippings and internet sites).

The field of research was extended beyond the traditional tourist resort areas to include respondents from a wide range of communities in all parishes. The sample for the survey was drawn from population data and demographic statistical publications of the Statistical Institute of Jamaica (STATIN) and the Planning Institute of Jamaica (PIOJ). These included the *Population Census* (1991), *the Economic and Social Survey of Jamaica* (1998 and 2000), as well as the *Statistical Abstract* (1998). The population was stratified into parishes and quota samples drawn from each to reflect the rural and urban distribution of residents and their demographic characteristics.

In the questionnaire survey, male and female respondents were more or less evenly distributed (see Figure 1.1) and there was a diverse mix of age

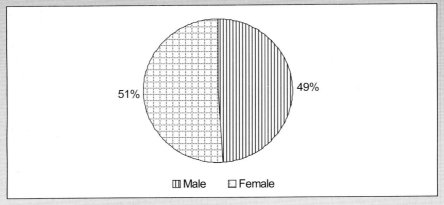

Figure 1.1   Sex Distribution of Respondents

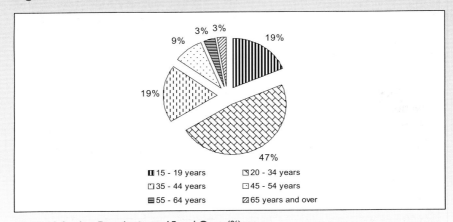

Figure 1.2   Age Distribution – 15 and Over (%)

ranges (see Figure 1.2), with an emphasis on younger members of the workforce.

This sample of the whole country reflects both the experiences of direct industry employees as well as other voices rarely heard on matters relating to this national industry. The important assumption informing the analysis is that tourism is everybody's business.

Key perceptions assessed were:

- who is a tourist
- tourists and their income status
- who benefits most and least from tourism
- how Jamaicans are treated in resort areas
- the main problems affecting the industry
- solutions to the problem of security in resort areas
- how the industry is managed
- sources of information on tourism messages

Definitions

The term 'attitude' as used in this study refers to the settled opinion or way of thinking of a person, as well as the behaviour reflecting this thinking. For ease of reference, the term is used interchangeably in different contexts with 'views', 'opinions' and 'perceptions'. It is assumed that the level of information available to the public is an important factor in the formation of attitudes. Attitudes, including behaviour, are influenced by other background factors such as age, sex, education, occupation and location of residence. In this context, attitudes and behaviour may be influenced by whether a respondent lives within or outside of a resort area or whether or not they depend on the industry for a living.

2

Popular Perceptions
of Tourism
Survey Results

This section presents the findings of the questionnaire survey. Specific issues are highlighted and the responses presented in narrative or tabular form.

Importance of tourism

People in selected communities all over the country were asked to give their opinions about the importance of tourism and how they felt about the industry. The results show that the majority of Jamaicans interviewed were very positive and supportive of tourism as a major plank in the economy (Figure 2.1). Some 86.4 percent of respondents regarded tourism as being very important to Jamaica, while 10.5 percent saw it as reasonably important. Only 3.1 percent saw it as not very important.

Economic benefits and dependence on tourism

This question on this issue tried to determine the extent to which people saw tourism as providing economic benefits, and the distinction people made

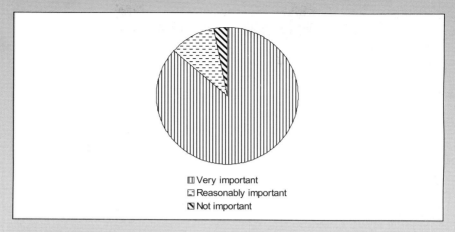

Figure 2.1 Importance of Tourism

between personal benefit, family benefit and national benefit. Thirty percent of respondents said that, at a personal level, they depended directly or indirectly on tourism for a living (Figure 2.2). In addition, 26 percent said that a member or members of their immediate family worked in tourism. This suggests that 56 percent of those sampled were either involved, or had family members who derived financial benefits from the industry. Naturally, a higher percentage of these respondents were found to be from traditional resort areas. The varying levels and extent of dependence was outside the scope of this study, but will need to be explored in further studies.

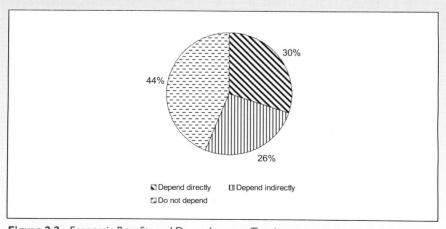

Figure 2.2 Economic Benefits and Dependence on Tourism

Perceptions of the financial benefits of tourism to the community

Although the previous findings suggest that many people depend on tourism to some extent, the perception of a significant portion of those interviewed is that tourism provides limited benefits to their communities. The largest group of respondents (38 percent) perceives tourism as not providing any benefits at this level. The second largest (36 percent) felt the impact was moderately beneficial. Only a quarter of the respondents (26 percent) felt that their community benefited a lot or reasonably well from tourism.

The results also show that age, gender and place of residence affected perceptions. The group that most strongly perceived the industry as bringing a lot of benefit to their community was older people (over 55 years old) living in parishes with tourist facilities. Those perceiving limited benefits were mainly females, while those reporting no benefits were people of both genders in the age range of 20–44 living outside of 'tourist areas'. There appears to be a higher expectation level among the younger respondents.

As expected, employment in the industry and residence within or outside a resort area strongly influenced perceptions. Persons employed in the industry or living in tourist resort areas perceived the industry as benefiting the community a lot, while those who were not employed in the sector or those who lived in non-resort areas understandably reported a lower level of community benefit.

Perception of primary beneficiaries

General perceptions of 'who benefits most' and 'who benefits least' were clear-cut. In general, there was a very strong view that it is the 'big man' who benefits most and the 'small man' who benefits least. The term 'big man' was most consistently associated with owners of large all-inclusive hotels, overseas travel companies, airline and cruise ship operators and owners of in-bond shops.

Those seen as deriving least benefit from the industry included small businesses, and local people. The most popular images of the 'small man' were small business people, such as some taxi operators, craft vendors, higglers, local farmers, and operators of local villas and guest houses, as well as low level workers in the industry.

Tourism as a priority sector

While a previous result indicated strong support for tourism as a very important sector, responses to this question show that it was not ranked as *the* priority sector to improve the economy and create more jobs (Figure 2.3).

Respondents were asked to rank in order of importance the three sectors on which they thought the country should place most emphasis. Analysis was based on the selection ranked as number one, as indicative of the dominant opinion. Almost half the respondents (48 percent) felt that Tourism should be the *second* most important sector (38 percent) after Agriculture (48 percent). In rank order, the remaining priority sectors were Manufacturing (30 percent), Information Technology (23 percent) and Bauxite (19 percent).

Gender, age and education also influenced perceptions of Tourism as the priority sector. Females, people over 45 years, and those with a secondary education or higher, were more likely to think it should be the main sector. Similarly, those who work in the industry or live in resort areas were more likely to see it as a priority sector than those who did not.

Manufacturing and Information Technology were seen (particularly among the young) as potentially important sectors for employment. No doubt, this relates to the existence of the Free Trade Zones and on-going government and private sector discussions in the media about expanding the Information Technology sector.

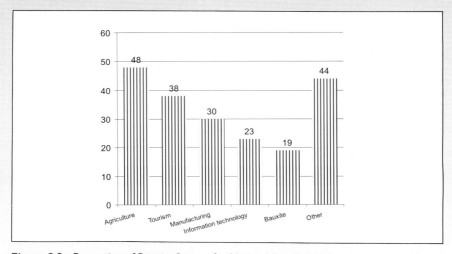

Figure 2.3 Perception of Priority Sectors for National Development

Perceptions of problems in the tourism industry

While it is generally understood that the industry has many difficulties, this question sought to determine people's perceptions of the three biggest problems. Analysis of frequency responses for the number one problem selected (Figure 2.4) showed that in rank order these were crime and violence (59.3 percent), bad roads (38.5 percent) and visitor harassment (29.1 percent).

Perceptions of other problems in rank order were: poor service (19.3 percent); too little people to people contact (16.5 percent); Inadequate distribution of attractions (16.2 percent); high unemployment (14 percent); overcharging (13.8 percent), and high prices (12.3 percent). The 'other' category had a frequency distribution of 28.0 percent, but it was not possible to analyse these responses further, because details were not provided.

Further analysis of the data for crime and violence as the number one problem, showed that while gender did not influence perceptions, several other factors did. These included education, age, and whether or not people depended on the industry for a living. Those perceiving crime and violence as the main problem were more likely to have post-secondary education, to be younger (in the 15–19 age group) and not dependent on tourism for a living. In contrast, those people working in the sector were less likely to see crime as a major problem.

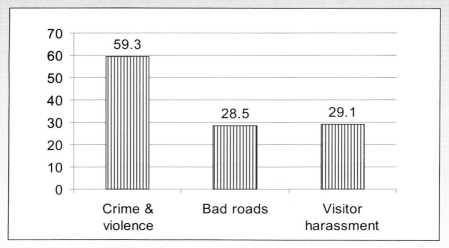

Figure 2.4 Perceptions of Industry Problems

More in-depth analysis was also done of visitor harassment, given the scale of the problem. Gender, age, education and employment in the sector and residence influenced perceptions of visitor harassment as the number one problem. Respondents in this category tended to have lower education, to be older, depended directly on tourism for a living, and were more likely to live on the North Coast.

Perceived solutions to the problem of security in resort areas

Interviewees were asked to indicate how they thought security could be improved in resort areas and to rank their responses in order of priority. Analysis of the frequency distribution of the number one solution selected, showed that most people felt that more community education was the most effective way to tackle the problem. This option had a frequency of 41 percent, and in rank order the other solutions were: better street lighting (35 percent); stiffer penalties for crimes (34.2 percent); better security information for tourists (32.5 percent); more police/resort patrols (32.0 percent); more soldiers (27.1 percent). The 'other' category had a frequency distribution of 55.8 percent but no further analysis was possible, as respondents did not elaborate.

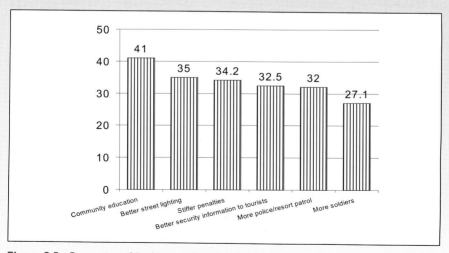

Figure 2.5 Perception of Soultions to Security Problems

These findings suggest that education and information to locals and tourists, combined with improved infrastructure (e.g. street lighting) could be effective solutions. In a separate category are stiffer penalties for harassers and better policing. Increasing the number of soldiers in resort areas was perceived as the least effective method of dealing with security problems.

In-depth analysis of respondents who saw community policing as the main strategy (priority number 1) showed that they were slightly more likely to be males, have post-secondary education, be over 45 years, depend indirectly or directly on tourism for a living, and live outside the resort areas. Figure 2.5 summarizes the main findings.

Perceived strategies to improve benefits from tourism

Interviewees were asked to rank the three most important changes they would like to see in the tourism sector that would bring more financial benefits to the Jamaican economy.

In rank order, the frequency responses for the number one priority selected were: using more local foods (57 percent), improving security in tourist areas (32 percent), improving roads (30 percent), promoting rural and environmental tourism (28 percent); improving training for people in tourism (27 percent); using fewer imported products – not only food (26 percent); and promoting more cultural and heritage tourism (21 percent). These attitudes were consistent with the view that agriculture should be the main economic sector for the country's development. They also reflect the concern about crime and violence as the main problem, and the widespread concern about poor roads. The other responses are consistent with previously discussed issues such as the view that the benefits of tourism were skewed in favour of the 'big man', with relatively few benefits accruing to communities. These responses confirm the need to diversify and expand the tourism product and to use more local foods and other products.

Persons who advocated using more local foods as the main priority were more likely to be male, with post-secondary education, older (45–54 years), directly dependent on tourism for a living, and living in a resort area. Those who recommended improving security forces in tourist areas were over 45 years old, less likely to depend on tourism for a living and more likely to live outside a resort area.

Perceptions of tourists

Respondents were asked to indicate the first picture that comes to mind when they think of a tourist. The most popular view, represented by nearly half of those interviewed (46.3 percent), is that tourists are visitors from overseas (Figure 2.6). Slightly more than a quarter (27.3 percent) saw them as people of all races. Only 19.2 percent saw them as 'white foreigners'. The remaining 7.2 percent saw them as guests in a resort hotel.

These findings are consistent with the qualitative data, and indicate a significant diversity of public perception of tourists. Some recognize them as people of all races. The fact that less than ten percent saw them as guests in a resort hotel suggests that most people do not see Jamaicans on holiday in resort areas as tourists.

Characteristics of two types of respondents were analysed in more detail. The group who saw them as visitors from overseas were more likely to be male, with higher education, in the 20–44 age range, with limited dependence on tourism for a living. They were also more likely to live in a resort area.

Those who saw them as white were more likely to be females, with post-secondary education, young (15–34 years old), not dependent on tourism for a living, and living outside of a resort area. These results help to identify areas for education, training and public education. No doubt, many may already be receiving attention through the JTB education and communications

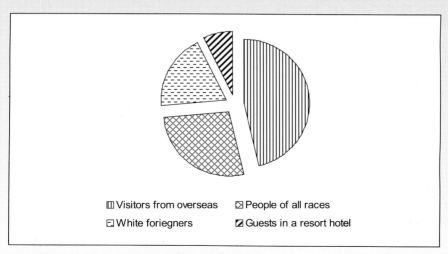

Figure 2.6 Jamaicans' Perceptions of Tourists (%)

programmes and well as the Tourism Product Development Company (TPDCo) training programmes.

Perceptions of tourists' financial status

In response to a question asking their perception of the financial status of tourists who come to Jamaica, the most common response was that most tourists are ordinary working people who save their money and come for a holiday (Table 2.1). Over half of those interviewed (54 percent) had this view. Another third (31 percent) saw tourists as well-off people with reasonable amounts of money to spend. Only 10 percent saw them as rich people with lots of money to spend. Five percent of respondents chose 'other' which usually indicated that Jamaica had a combination of the other categories of tourists mentioned.

Table 2.1 Perceptions of Tourists' Financial Status

Responses	Percentage
Ordinary people	54
Well-off people	31
Rich people	10
Other	5
Total	100

Source: Dunn and Dunn (Survey data)

Contact with tourists

Based on the premise that attitudes are often shaped by personal experiences, the study tried to determine how many of those interviewed had actually met and talked with a tourist. The results show that a quarter of those Jamaicans interviewed (25 percent) had no contact with tourists. The remaining 75 percent had had some contact at some time in their lives. While this figure may be understood in the context of respondents' lifetime experience, it may also be considered a high proportion relative to the distribution of resorts. The field staff considered that some respondents may have answered in the affirmative to enhance their image. In any event, expanding opportunities for direct contact between visitors and residents is likely to improve attitudes to visitors.

Those who said they had met a tourist to talk to were more likely to be male, with either no education or a post-secondary education. Age was not a factor influencing the likelihood of contact. Understandably those who work in the industry have more access than those who do not. Similarly, those who live in a resort area are more likely to have contact compared to those who live elsewhere.

Influence of tourists on life in Jamaica

Respondents were asked to indicate the main ways that tourists influence life in Jamaica. The most frequent responses for the number one priority selected (Table 2.2) were money (83 percent), building friendships (19.4 percent) and negative values (10 percent). The results also suggest that tourists were seen as transmitting more negative values (10 percent) than positive ones (7.5 percent). This perception is related to lifestyle issues such as use of illegal drugs and prostitution. (Total percentages exceed 100 as they relate to frequency of responses to each given category.)

Table 2.2   Perceptions of Tourists' Influence on Jamaica

Perceptions of Main Influence	Frequency (%)
Bring money	83
Build friendships	19
Other	19
Negative values	10
Bring culture	9
Drugs	7.8
Positive values	7.5
Prostitution	5.8

Source: Dunn and Dunn (Survey data)

Treatment of Jamaicans in resort hotels

Perceptions of the treatment of Jamaicans on vacation in comparison to foreign tourists were predominantly negative. Almost one-half (49.1 percent) perceived Jamaicans as receiving worse treatment than overseas visitors receive, while approximately one-third (32.5 percent) felt they were treated the same (see Figure 2.7). Another 4.5 percent felt they would be treated better, while 13.9 percent said they did not know.

Sources of information on tourism

Interviewees were asked to indicate whether they knew which agency had the main responsibility for the administration and development of tourism. The response rate to this question was very high. More than half of those interviewed (54.7 percent) said they either did not know or were not sure what the agency was. However, a significant 45.3 percent said they knew. Of those who knew, more than three-quarters (81 percent) named the Jamaica Tourist Board as that agency. This indicates a reasonable presence of the JTB in the public's eye. However, there is need to increase public awareness of the Board and its work among the 54.7 percent who either did not know or were not sure.

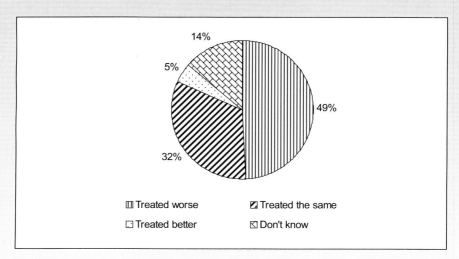

Figure 2.7   Treatment of Jamaicans in Resort Areas

The other tourism related agencies and individuals named, accounted for 13 percent of responses. These included: Prime Minister P.J. Patterson, the Ministry of Tourism and the Minister of Tourism and the Jamaica Hotel and Tourist Association (JHTA). Air Jamaica, Sandals and Butch Stewart were also mentioned. Six percent of responses did not relate to the tourism industry but to other institutions (e.g. Planning Institute of Jamaica and government ministries).

There is some public confusion about the range of agencies responsible for aspects of tourism management. Competing conceptions range from the JTB (predominant) to the Office of the Prime Minister. In the more recent survey phase, there was a higher level of association with the Minister of Tourism, but still some confusion around the respective roles of the Ministry and the JTB. The integration or streamlining of responsibilities would contribute to the presentation of a stronger image of agency responsibility and coherence in the management of the sector.

Sources of tourism messages

Interviewees were asked if they could remember seeing or hearing specific advertisements in Jamaica about tourism. Seventy percent said they had (see Figure 2.8). Of these, the most frequently mentioned sources were television (65.3 percent) and radio (11.1 percent). The high level of response for television is likely to include local viewing of overseas based cable channels.

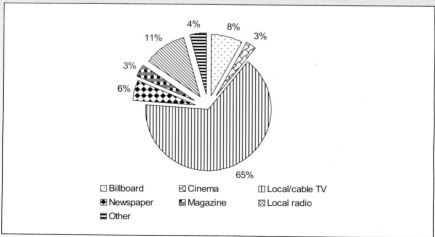

Figure 2.8 Sources of Tourism Advertisement

Tourism messages

The most frequently remembered messages were: "Don't harass the tourist," "Come to Jamaica and feel alright/One love, One heart," "Spring break" and "Reggae Boys".

The responses can be interpreted in several ways. To provide broad options for decision-making each is outlined: 34 percent of the entire sample named the JTB as the source of these messages. Among those who said they knew the agency putting out the message, 71 percent named the JTB.

Media and listenership

Jamaican audiences through various media outlets received tourism messages. When asked to rank the radio stations listened to most respondents indicated IRIE FM, FAME FM, RJR Supreme Sound, Radio 2, Hot 102, LOVE FM, Power 106 and KLAS FM in that order. Few people among the national sample had access to community radio stations and the largest listenership in this group was to Roots FM. In television, the level of viewing between CVM and TVJ was almost equal, but CVM had the edge. Love TV's viewership was small but significant in urban centres.

Cable viewing

Sixty one percent of those interviewed said that they watched cable. More than half of these respondents (55.2 percent), indicated that they watched more foreign cable channels than local TV channels.

Newspaper choices

Findings confirmed the top newspapers in rank order as *The Gleaner, The Observer, The Star, X News* and *The Sunday Herald*. Those who read community newspapers were spread across a variety of local community publications, including *The Mirror* and *The News*.

Synopsis

The results of the survey are likely to contribute to a better understanding of Jamaican views, perceptions and attitudes relating to tourism. An important message flowing from the data is the need for internal restructuring of the industry to ensure a greater role for the less privileged part of the population in the industry. The artisans, small transport operators and vendors need to see themselves as having a stake in the future of Jamaican tourism. There is also need for greater public education about the overall contribution of tourism to the economy. Whereas the lion's share of promotional resources has been placed in overseas advertising, there is also an urgent need for greater resource allocation to in-country public education, as well as training of hotel employees.

Among other approaches flowing from the responses is the need to initiate a collective review of the communication strategies of key tourism agencies and to develop an integrated communication programme for the industry. At the same time, the findings strongly suggest that improved communication strategies and more effective messages will not by themselves improve attitudes to tourism or tourists, or build a stronger stakeholder base for tourism to flourish. In order to address perceptions of alienation and inequitable distribution of industry benefits, there is a pressing need to restructure the industry itself, to reduce the number of layers of management and expand community and small business involvement in tourism. Greater efforts should be made to encourage more active partnerships between all-inclusive hotels and local businesses, in order to expose hotel guests to more Jamaican attractions in the community.

Poverty eradication, infrastructure improvements (roads, affordable housing, streetlights, etc.) and urban redevelopment initiatives were also considered critical to the continued success of the industry. Similarly, programmes of public education, skill training and employment creation must complement existing efforts to improve the tourism product.

The industry in Jamaica must be seen as not just consisting of resort pockets or 'tourist areas' but as an integrated national industry, linked to agriculture, music and the creative arts. People felt strongly that government, private sector and NGO partnerships should be developed and strengthened to increase the variety and spread of attractions beyond traditional resort areas. It is only with this approach that the authorities will be able to successfully tackle the pressing problems of security, harassment and hostility by those alienated from the benefits of the industry.

CHAPTER 3

Talking Tourism
Focus Group Discussions

While the foregoing chapters present a broad national overview of opinions and attitudes to tourism, the group discussions, meetings and specialist interviews offer greater depth, context and specificity. These qualitative research methods probed for explanations of views and sought to establish linkages among the wide range of attitudes unearthed. It is through this varied, close and direct dialogue that we are able to gain deeper insights into the attitudes of Jamaicans towards the industry.

The results from the in-depth dialogue provide substantial validation for the findings of the questionnaire survey and introduce important additional elements into the analysis.

The full range of qualitative methods used were:

- Focus group discussions
- Community meetings
- Dialogue with youth groups and school children
- Participant observation of the tourism planning process
- Interviews with selected stakeholders and sector leaders

Table 3.1: Focus Group Summary

Group	Location	# Participants
Unemployed Youth	Flankers	6
Craft Vendors	Ocho Rios	9
Craft Vendors	Montego Bay	12
Rural Youth	Windsor Castle	6
Rural Citizens	Sligoville	5
Hotel Managers	Ocho Rios	5
Taxi Operators	Caymanas	8
Residents	Treasure Beach	9
Inner-city Youth	Kingston	9
Total		69

Source: Dunn and Dunn (Survey data)

All focus group leaders and community meeting facilitators used common guidelines for eliciting the main attitudes and key issues among participants. However, while the focus group leaders concentrated the discussions on specific themes, the community meetings took a more free-flowing form. They relied more on the issues brought to the table by the residents, provided those issues were within the general framework of the study.

Nine focus group sessions were conducted. Table 3.1 provides an overview of their composition, location and the number of participants.

Focus group reports

Unemployed youth in Flankers, St James

The Flankers area is a densely populated, depressed and sometimes volatile community on the outskirts of the main resort town of Montego Bay. The community overlooks the Donald Sangster International Airport and is located on the main North Coast road linking urban Montego Bay to other resort neighbourhoods such as Rose Hall and Ironshore. This main highway is also the essential artery linking Montego Bay to Ocho Rios and Kingston.

The focus group discussion in this community was held one week after a demonstration in the community which caused the blockage of the main highway as well as severe inconvenience to normal commuter traffic and airport shuttle services for tourists (Smith 1999).

The focus group consisted of six male residents of the area. Four participants were in the 18 to 25 age range and two were more mature men in their mid-thirties. All were unemployed and lived by 'hustling' and mutual support. One of the youths was a student at a tertiary level institution.

The main attitude evident in the group was resentment at what they regarded as acute neglect of their community. They said that attention was paid to their area only when there was a demonstration or major incident. They felt strongly that the tourism industry was organized for the wealthy in society, whom they also saw as mainly white or 'brown' people.

The eldest member of the group said: "Tourism leave out the vendors, craft people, ghetto youths and poor people in general." Expressing agreement with this, another member complained that the police were the ones who were harassing ghetto youths when they tried to reason with tourists. In response to questions about youths harassing tourists, one of the younger and more aggressive members of the group declared: "More time tourists fi get harass, and rob too, cause a nuff time dem rob we abroad and trick we. Right yah now in Jamaica, nuff a dem tell lie pon youth say youth and youth tief dem. Anything tourist say people tek as right and truth; no investigation!" While some others in the group nodded their support, one member expressed disagreement with robbing tourists and an argument ensued.

The student in the group explained that the Flankers area did not benefit much from tourism although it was in the middle of the Montego Bay tourism area: "People from Flankers who work in the industry affi give wrong address." He said there was no training nor were there employment opportunities for men or women. Because of neglect and deprivation, many people had become hostile to outsiders and aggressive towards the visitors.

The group was asked to explain their understanding of the reason tourists came to Jamaica and the financial status of most visitors. All members said they had met tourists to talk to and that many visitors approached them for ganja or cocaine. They said some male tourists whom they met in this way introduced them to female tourists who wanted sex for money. The majority in the group was of the view that "tourists have money". The degree of wealth did not seem to matter. One participant felt that "even the poorest tourist have more money than we the ghetto youth".

Regarding suggestions for improvement in their condition and in their relationship with the industry, the group members appealed for more jobs: "We can do any work, even taxi or water sport. Every day we go out to look work, but nutten. We need some training, cause we no really love the gun business. We born ya and we haffi survive one way or another. We need fi get some help."

Asked about their attitudes to any tourism messages they may have heard, the eldest member of the group observed that although government said they put people first, in tourism "dem put white people first".

In summary, the group of young, unemployed men in Flankers were of the view that:

- they and their families are grossly neglected, stigmatized and victimized;
- there is a strong feeling of hostility to most authority structures among some youth who were willing to exploit the industry in whatever legal or illegal ways they could;
- they were willing to work, to receive training and to cooperate if efforts were made to provide some form of assistance to them and their community.

Some of the young men in the Flankers group noted ominously that they were in control of an essential strategic location in the layout of the resort communities of the island. They live very close to the centre of the major resort area, with many important resort properties nearby. Their community is on one of the main routes to the Sangster International Airport and the main North Coast highway from Montego Bay to Ocho Rios and Kingston. Their actions could create major dislocations if they again reacted with demonstrations in response to their perception of continued neglect.

At the same time, many of these youth did not appear to possess the basic educational preparation and social skills to be readily absorbed in the industry. The need for education and training was evident as one route out of the deprivation expressed by the participants. Their threat of direct action on the street is a real one and reflects the vulnerability of the industry and of those resort communities where such sharp social and economic disparities were juxtaposed.

Craft vendors – Montego Bay and Ocho Rios

Two focus group meetings with craft vendors took place, one in the Montego Bay (Harbour Street) Craft Market and the other in the Ocho Rios Craft Market. Mixed groups of male and female vendors participated, with a majority of women taking part. In Ocho Rios 9 vendors participated and in the larger Montego Bay meeting there were 12. In both cases, key leaders of the Craft Vendors Associations took part in the discussion. Care was taken to ensure that the Association's leaders were not directly involved in the selection of other participants for the focus group discussions.

Vendors in both resort areas felt that they were treated as a "second class" subsector in terms of access to the tourists and availability of assistance to develop their products. One vendor in Ocho Rios said the craft people were like "country cousins" to the in-bond stores and large hotels where access to visitors and government assistance with promotion were concerned: "Government help the big hotel operators with advertising and overseas promotion. They must also help us more to advertise the craft industry as an attraction, not just as a market." Other participants in that discussion group agreed. Similar sentiments had also emerged in the Montego Bay meeting.

The focus group leader probed to see whether there were deeply held attitudes of dependency among the vendors. It became clear that some were willing to pay their own way as far as possible, but wanted the specialist marketing expertise and international connections required. One Montego Bay vendor remarked: "We will pool to help pay for some of the advertising but we need expert help and contacts." However, more than half of the participants in the same meeting saw the tasks of promotion and product upgrading as the responsibility of government. They said that they are paying rents, which were quite high, and that they needed more direct assistance with marketing.

In the Montego Bay focus group, vendors suggested that large operators in the accommodations sector were unfairly taking over craft vending, putting specialists like themselves out of business. They said that the big hotels were establishing larger and larger craft stores within the hotel premises. They argued that some of these products were bought cheaply from local tradesmen and wholesalers and later retailed at inflated prices to the tourist.

Other participants agreed. They explained that since most of the tourists from all-inclusive hotels were not taken to the outside craft markets, these visitors did not know what other Jamaican crafts were available. Neither did the visitors have a wide choice in prices and products. One participant claimed that sometimes even imported craft items and clothing were sold as Jamaican goods in some establishments.

Vendors in the Montego Bay craft market also acknowledged the assistance they received from government in upgrading the market. However, they wished to see a greater flow in tourist traffic into the market. Many complained bitterly about the cost of rent compared to weekly or monthly sales.

The vendors in both markets remarked on what they saw as a significant reduction in aggressive and competitive behaviour towards visitors. They attributed this to some training from TPDCo and to a better recognition that harassment of patrons was already turning off the flow of visitors into the markets. A male member of the Ocho Rios group said: "We exercise more control now over people in the market who a try to rush the tourists." The participants considered this an important attitude change among stall owners, supported by their Associations. They want more on-going, direct training programmes to help maintain this.

In Montego Bay, vendors felt that outside the market, harassment was getting worse, combined with direct robbery and assault of visitors. "Tourists can't walk free on account of unemployed youth from poor and run down areas in the town. Somebody should go into Canterbury, Flankers, Railway Lane and North Gully areas and try to work with the youths and provide some jobs and training," said one leader of the Association. She explained that although these people lived so close to the luxury of the industry, they felt they were not benefiting from it.

Most participants in both the Montego Bay and Ocho Rios discussions agreed that:

- Hotel operators should stick mainly to accommodation and not establish craft markets or arcades inside of their 'all-inclusive' properties or big hotels.
- Craft items sold to tourists in Jamaica should not be imported, but should be the handiwork of Jamaicans who need the jobs and income.
- Craft markets should be promoted as attractions, not just as markets. Promotional assistance should be provided to the craft sector in the same way that assistance was sometimes given to large hotels and major events. Vendors agreed that they would also contribute to this expanded promotion.

- Harassment was not just a poor-man or small business activity: "Some of the in-bond merchants a employ pimps fi harass tourists fi come inna dem store too," was a comment from one participant in the Ocho Rios discussion.
- The use of armed soldiers in the resort areas was not desirable. Vendors were in favour of using more police on foot patrols and in the bicycle squads.
- Better public education, more training of industry employees and more jobs were needed, especially for the young people in the resort capitals and surrounding towns.

Rural youth – Windsor Castle, Portland

The Windsor Castle focus group meeting was held with the participation of six young people: three young men and three young women all between the ages of 17 and 26 years. Most were self-employed. The main issues emerging were their frustration with the limited opportunities for employment within the community.

Some were of the view that with better organization, communities like theirs could benefit more from tourism. "Mark" (not his real name) participated actively in the Neighborhood Watch and had lobbied to get the roads fixed properly. He and his group were also trying to organize a community newspaper and were involved in eco-tourism. Mark also worked as a tour guide, providing services to European tourist groups each year, taking them on mountain trails in Portland. He reported that he had already secured bookings for two years in advance.

Other members of the group, in sharp contrast, felt that it was the government's responsibility to provide jobs and solutions. Two members of the group frequently visited Ocho Rios in search of work. Sometimes they made and sold craft items to in-bond shops and hotels. Sales were slow, however, and the returns very low.

In discussing the impact of tourism on Jamaica, some strong views emerged about the problem of illegal drugs. Most were of the view that narcotics had a negative impact on the tourism industry. The problem was regarded as being more serious in Ocho Rios. One participant said this problem could easily be solved "if the Ocho Rios police did their job properly; they know where the drug dons are and where the drugs are sold and could close down the operations if they wanted to". This popular perception of the attitude of some police personnel reflected concerns in several resort areas.

The young people were also upset at how the police addressed ordinary people: "Police should talk to people with respect and encourage them. They should not use so much violence against people who they find hustling for a living."

One female participant also wanted clarification on what the government does with the money earned from tourism, because she could not see how the community benefited. During the discussion, it was also pointed out that tourism not only benefited Jamaicans, but also gave opportunities to tourists to pursue their own businesse: "Some buy land and set up business here, because they love the country."

Their suggestions to improve tourism were:

- more organized attempts to assist small operators who are trying to make a contribution to the industry;
- greater attention to agriculture and its linkage into employment and tourism;
- greater efforts by the police to eliminate drug dealings in Ocho Rios and other areas and thereby help to clean up the image of tourism;
- special attention to the plight of young, unemployed women, particularly in the rural areas;
- more of the money earned from tourism to be ploughed back in communities like theirs to address their needs.

Older rural citizens – Sligoville, St Catherine

This focus group included a middle-aged shopkeeper, a female householder and three younger men in the community, a total of five participants. This discussion helped to identify opportunities for rural communities to benefit from tourism.

The shopkeeper noted that tourists come by when the 'River Road' was blocked. They stop, buy Red Stripe beer (especially the Italians) and ask the name of plants and fruits. They beg for mangoes and ask about the community. "No people not up here to harass them, so they make themselves at home . . . and ask to use the bathroom."

The following views were shared about tourism as a major national sector. One participant observed that "tourism is not a mus' and we can't force this.

Fix up the place right and leave them to come and enjoy it and we would get more [from it]." There was also the view that Jamaica was "calling on tourism too much and the industry is going down. We should diversify to increase benefits . . . only big people benefiting right now . . . little people not benefiting at all . . . but the little man need to improve himself."

The female householder pointed out that younger people have a negative attitude to tourists and abuse tourists without a reason: ". . . call them 'whitey' . . . they only thinking about quick money nowadays . . ."

The solution? "The younger generation need to be educated about why some tend to harass tourists . . . they need to understand the money it brings . . . and to see how they benefit indirect." This participant bemoaned the fact that "there is too much killing of tourists . . . they need more protection . . . [but] police also need to give better treatment to local people . . ."

The shopkeeper felt that those in charge of the industry were "doing a lousy job" because "they are poor at protecting the tourist". Their community, for example, was peaceful and quiet, had good roads and little crime, but had few attractions.

Suggestions to expand tourism opportunities in that area included:
- promoting the Sligoville Great House where the first slaves who were set free were reportedly brought;
- training youth to be tour guides and exposing them to different parts of the country;
- educating young people about Jamaican culture;
- promoting local drinks, foods and other local attractions; developing water supply and electricity services faster throughout the adjoining communities.

Senior industry employees and hotel managers – Ocho Rios

The focus group meeting was held at the Roman Catholic Church in Ocho Rios. Five persons participated, comprising two males and three females. The majority of participants were senior managers in large hotels operating in the Ocho Rios area. Job functions included a franchise holder/manager, a human resource manager, a senior housekeeper, the proprietor of a gift shop located within a hotel property, and a minister of religion whose church members worked in a variety of occupations within the industry.

Findings from the discussion are summarized as follows:

Perceptions of tourism

Jamaica as a tourist destination can be described as 'a paradise' but its impact is being compromised by certain developments. There was insufficient government investment. This was evidenced by poor infrastructure, insufficient information and education about tourism for schools and the general public. There were also inadequate amenities for tourism workers. One group member highlighted a lack of housing and poor transportation services as very acute problems which affected the productivity, attitude and comfort of workers. Rent was very high for local residents and any new accommodation being built was for tourists only. It was stated that the majority of hotel workers were not benefiting enough from the National Housing Trust loan facility as their salaries were too low to allow them to qualify.

Some participants noted that environmental pollution was very serious, especially of the rivers and sea. This was compounded by poor sanitation and solid waste disposal systems in Ocho Rios. There was inadequate sensitivity to the fragility of the tourism industry and the environment and how they could be protected: "Tourism is not fostered, but is rather allowed to happen," one participant observed.

All participants regarded tourist harassment as a major problem. They felt it was heavily influenced by the lack of employment opportunities for local people. Therefore, the all-inclusive properties had become the norm as "it was neither safe nor comfortable for tourists to experience Jamaica outside the hotels". A female group member said that involvement of local people in tourism must be organized and planned. For example, hair braiders should operate from special shops with guidelines for the trade. This would reduce the problem of harassment. Currently, the braiders harass the tourists for business and the police harass the braiders.

Some participants felt that most of our tourist resorts were not friendly. The social and economic deprivation of local people made it difficult for them to both appreciate and participate in tourism. There was too sharp a contrast between the facilities for tourists and those for local residents. For example, tourists travel in air conditioned buses while local transportation was almost nonexistent in many resort areas and neighbouring parishes.

More generally, it was felt that while local people were directly affected by the problems and developments in tourism, they were not participants in determining the solutions. The potential of the local population was not being exploited by the tourism industry. Training was essential to equip workers in the industry with the appropriate attitudes and skills. Particular reference was made to craft vendors. It was felt that government should provide more training for them to achieve product diversification and improved quality.

Benefits from tourism

The group identified a wide range of benefits being derived from the industry. These included tax payments to the Jamaican government from tourists, workers and the hotels. Tourists made in-bond and other purchases, and the industry was a major earner of foreign exchange. It enabled diverse cultural exchanges – food, music, dance and other cultural forms were showcased. This was seen as good because "visitors also want to experience more than sand, sea and sun". In addition, the industry was a major source of employment. People from a wide geographical area came to work in Ocho Rios. A worker could almost double his or her wages by gratuities, depending on the property and time of year. This compared very well with salaries of teachers and other professionals. Working in the tourism industry, one member said, "raised the expectations of workers and opened their eyes to how to live".

It was pointed out that opportunities for niche marketing in tourism existed and marketing tours to church groups overseas was one such opportunity. The church was involved in tourism, as cruise ship and other visitors attended services in resort areas at times and often stayed for activities afterwards.

Tourism advertising

Participants felt that 'word of mouth' was a major factor in tourism advertising. The high number of repeat guests, personal references and the fact that they brought other persons to visit, underscored the effectiveness of this form of advertising. They also said repeat business was strongly influenced by the quality of service and, more importantly, the attitudes of workers.

It was suggested that government needed to put more money into advertising, and to advertise earlier and more consistently in the relevant markets. The JTB advertisements were rated as very attractive with effective images. Advertisements depicting warm weather in winter in the appropriate places were rated as having great impact.

Physical and social infrastructure

Participants highlighted several issues considered detrimental to the effectiveness and quality of the tourism product. These annoyed some managers and made them apologetic about poor service. All were very interested in and committed to tourism. They wanted to see it develop and progress and were very confident that the Jamaican product was superior to most others. They felt, however, that the government had neglected to give it the attention and resources it deserved.

Among other problems identified were poor infrastructure and utilities. Bad roads and poor transportation were burning issues especially in resort areas. These infrastructural problems significantly demotivated both tourists and local people. Unreliable electricity supply in Ocho Rios often caused discomfort and inconvenience. In addition, there was poor service at the airport, with customs and immigration personnel regarded as very slow, inefficient and sometimes unfriendly. Other tourist destinations provide far superior airport service. There were inadequate restroom facilities generally, including in the resort areas. Tourists go out all day but have limited access to rest rooms. The group noted that the incidence of men urinating in public would be reduced with the provision of accessible rest rooms.

On the matter of security, it was observed that some guests were scared to venture outside of hotel properties because of ignorance, fear of harassment and theft in some areas. Limited environmental and other attractions are inhibiting factors on return visits. The lack of a marine park in Ocho Rios was also noted. In addition, health care facilities were inadequate for both local residents and visitors.

The following suggestions emerged out of the discussion:

- More education about the industry must be provided in schools from the primary level, to reduce harassment and engender a good attitude to tourism.
- Increase in government's tourism advertising budget and provision of incentives for investors to participate in providing the needed amenities, such as housing for tourism workers.
- The need for Jamaica to regain the high-end of the tourism market which has been lost to other destinations. The diversification of the market is good but it must not be at the expense of the high-end groups. The influx of spring-breakers was not seen as the way to develop the market; rather it

was viewed as signaling a depreciation of high-end properties, which traditionally catered to more mature and well-established tourists.

- Adjusting prices in the all-inclusive properties closer to those of small hotels placed the latter at a disadvantage. However, some small, well-known franchises such as Comfort Suites were doing well.
- Investment in public health facilities was considered a good prospect, and an urgent need, given the volume of tourists to Ocho Rios, the current lack of facilities and the potential to offer high quality health services to retirees. They would, however, need to be assured of efficient and prompt health services. This is an area in which the private sector could collaborate with government for the good of the sector.
- Protection from pollution and maintenance of the physical attractions of baths and waterfalls in and around Ocho Rios . They are considered to be among the best in the world and are regarded as being among the 'hottest items' internationally.
- The need for good restaurants outside of the hotel properties.
- The need to continue training programmes. A major plus for the industry is its excellent staff. Most recruitment should be done from the Human Employment and Resource Training Trust/National Training Academy (HEART/NTA).
- The need to continue education programmes. The JTB Tourism Quiz competition was lauded as an excellent programme and should be expanded to include hotels.

Rural taxi operators – Caymanas and Waterloo, St Catherine

This focus group discussion was conducted with eight participants. Six were taxi operators who transported passengers between Spanish Town and the Sligoville/Bog Walk areas, and two other participants worked as caddies in the nearby Caymanas Golf Club.

The discussion mainly reflected the thinking and attitude of representatives of the transport sector in a rural, non-tourist area. Although attempts were made to focus the discussion on issues of tourism, the participants explained their positions from concerns about their local conditions and rural experiences. However, they saw the prospect of tourism spreading to their area and had ideas about how parts of rural St Catherine could benefit from tourism.

There was considerable anger at the government authorities, frustration with the "taxation on small people" and the limited opportunities for earning a living. The taxi operators said they were disgusted with what they described as "oppression" against "white plate taxis", whose owners were only trying to make a living.

The view was expressed that "a feasibility study on unemployment was as important as doing a study on tourism". A survey like that would help to identify the number of youths who were out of work, what they can do, and to find a job to give them ". . . so they don't mash down what you are trying to do". In terms of local investment, one contributor referred to a lack of trust of government. He regarded this as an obstacle to investment. According to him, "People don't want to put up their money without government putting theirs up front first."

Several ideas emerged on how to create employment, spread the possible benefits of tourism to rural communities and improve the lives of ordinary citizens. These ideas are listed below:

- Solve the problems of illiteracy which is a major factor causing frustration and limited opportunities for employment. (One angry and articulate man in his 30s said he "trembled" whenever he had to write his name, and that he needed assistance in improving his literacy and educational level.)
- Develop local infrastructure in Spanish Town. Fix the roads and drains and organize more recreational facilities for residents first. (One person said, "There is no night life in Spanish Town.")
- Build more factories to provide employment because "when a youth see tourists spending money, him get red eye".
- Fix up Hellshire and the Forum Hotel to accommodate tourists to the benefit of Portmore.
- Encourage people to set up small guest houses in the community.
- Develop the Rio Cobre river for rafting and organize forest tours, using guides who know the area.
- Establish more local food stops (like those at Faith's Pen) as part of tours to expose visitors to tasty local cuisine.
- Help the community to form a group to organize tourism projects in the area.

Residents of Treasure Beach, St Elizabeth

The focus group meeting took place at Treasure Beach in St Elizabeth, with nine participants. These included an employee at a villa, three other local business people, two adult members of a Jamaican family, an England-based Jamaican visitor, a taxi operator and a fisherman who sometimes took tourists sightseeing.

Some participants complained about bad roads and poor water supply in the area. While Treasure Beach was small and had only a limited incidence of crime, there is a need to stem and control this effectively. The police based in Pedro Plains tended to come "only when something has happened". Residents said that sometimes when they called, the response was that no vehicle was available.

The participant from the UK was unclear about how hotel rates were applied: "When you go into hotels there is a problem. I bet you that Jamaicans living here will get a different rate from me." This is clearly an area of concern. "Am I a Jamaican or a foreign tourist? This thing about a Jamaican rate does not apply in some areas. It needs clarification. When my children came here last time there was misunderstanding. There are some who travel with their Jamaican passports although they also have a British passport."

A taxi driver stated that he benefited from tourism but that new arrangements imposed by the government would affect this negatively: "I benefit from tourism now a little and I have a car but the government is bringing in some arrangement involving a licence and a sign . . ." Several participants remarked that the industry was not distributing its benefits widely enough as the returns were controlled by "a few rich men".

Participants felt that the relaxing atmosphere and tranquility of Treasure Beach should be preserved and promoted. The view of a visiting Jamaican was that Treasure Beach or this part of St Elizabeth was under-promoted: "We have come here, seen a batch of tourists come by, spent a night and simply left for Negril. We like Treasure Beach and will always come here". One group member felt that Negril was given vastly more attention. The attraction owner said:

> If you want to come here you must ask yourself, what are you coming for? Is it just peace and quiet? The place needs to be promoted for what it is. The tranquility of Treasure Beach should be emphasized to attract those who want a quiet destination. We are not getting the real spenders. The ones who come are low

spenders. We have been promised development and promotion of the south coast but we haven't seen much.

Among the suggestions were the following, which called on the JTB to:

- provide more information about itself and make its activities more visible;
- erect better signs so that tourists can find their way around;
- organize monthly meetings with community groups, including the Neighbourhood Watch and provide more information on security problems in its campaign to make tourists more aware;
- use more local media to offer more information about the role of tourism, and about matters relevant to the development of the industry. Many people listen to radio and some still watched local (Jamaican) television;
- market Jamaica more aggressively to other overseas groups even though North Americans were now the main target group for our overseas marketing;
- provide more information on the government's new arrangements for taxi operators;
- clarify the policy on how special hotel rates were applied for Jamaicans and Jamaicans visiting from overseas, as well as the prices in which currencies were quoted;
- increase marketing to Jamaican communities overseas and vary packages to allow these guests to combine visits with relatives staying in a hotel;
- train drivers of tour buses in the history and culture of Jamaica. Encourage them to mix more with tourists when they stop for lunch rather than have both groups eating separately;
- spend more tourism earnings on promotion, road improvement.

Inner city youth – Kingston

Participants in this session were drawn from a cultural group whose members were from Kingston's inner city communities. The discussion was held at the offices of the Area Youth Foundation in downtown Kingston. Fifteen persons participated in the session. There were eight males and seven females, all in their late teens and early twenties. The group used Theatre in Education (TIE) as animation for community development. The project has produced a major theatre production, "Beatification of Area Boy", written by Nigerian author and playwright Wole

Soyinka, staged at the Ward Theatre in 1996. Since then, they have been involved in other productions both locally and overseas.

Their overall attitudes to tourists were positive. They felt that it was "nice to see people from different countries coming to visit Jamaica". Some members of the group had encountered tourists in inner city Kingston: "They ask a lot of questions and ask for directions . . . but youths get upset about dem taking pictures." Their images of tourists included: "someone walking around with a camera, asking a lot of questions". Others felt tourists were "high-colour people with an accent". A white woman walking downtown, another said, is likely to be seen as "rich, which made some people feel to start mobbing her". This shows that there is the assumption that if they are white and foreign they have money. "Dark skinned tourists have a better chance of getting around without harassment". Another member stated that "one bad experience of a tourist sends thousands [of them] away". "Foreign people's experience makes them afraid . . . they have one thing on their minds – you have come to harass them . . ." Then there is the information they get about Jamaica: "News reporters pick out all the negatives, and that lets tourists get afraid." A dilemma was then presented: "If we Jamaicans try to be friendly to tourists, other people say we are harassing them or selling them drugs . . . They shouldn't use one person to judge all of us." This group felt that "Jamaicans should be free to ask tourists about their country without police harassing us."

There was also recognition that "some people [are] not used to tourists . . . tourists should be treated in a good way . . . they should be comfortable around you, so they will come back. Then they will go out and tell other people about how beautiful it is here . . ." The problem was seen as people who were ". . . not educated about how to market tourism . . . to know enough about tourism and how they can help the economy. Some don't know and some don't care . . ." Another youth said, "In non-tourist areas, people treat them [tourists] good . . . friendly . . ." One member suggested that ". . . they should carry them into some other communities and see how people would treat them".

Participants also had views on how the problems could be addressed. "It's not expensive . . . educate people in tourist areas. They could ask our group to prepare skits to educate the public in tourist areas . . . We can do skits and give free shows. However, it has to be on a monthly basis or every two months, to soak . . . You don't need to use book and pencil . . ."

They were asked how they think their own community could benefit more from tourism. One participant mentioned the fact that the building they occupied was once a saltfish factory. They could find out more about it and prepare plays. Others suggested doing guided tours to inner-city communities for people who wanted it. In the past, they have provided "escort service for Peace Corps [personnel]".

They reminisced about life in the city. Feelings of isolation were also strong in the group: "We are an island to ourself. When Oceana [Hotel] was operating, people used to walk with us all over the city." Now things are very different.

Some suggested that it was possible to do research on how people in the ghetto live, talk, communicate and share this with others. The group felt that any solutions to the problem of tourism "must start in schools . . . the children would come home and share the information with their brothers and sisters and their parents. They should also use humour."

Perceptions of who benefits most from tourism varied. Some felt that it "helps all of us because we get foreign exchange". Others, however, saw it differently: "I don't see how it help us or wey di money go." It was felt that "they should use money from tourism to create other jobs". The need to spread the benefits of tourism more widely across the country was also raised. "Why not have Spring Break in other parishes – not just in one set place?"

The discussion also focused on solutions, and in this context the need for training was raised: "They should build up more places like HEART." Government's priorities for expenditure were also questioned. Some felt

> . . . government wasting money building unnecessary police station rather than factories . . . and too much money spen' on buses. Yout' don't have nothing to do, so dem crush a ends and tek up a gun. But dem don't want to do it . . . Look how dem spen' 10 million fi a promote a football an important tings like marl for di road and food for poor people not getting attention.

The reference to the "football" related to a JTB overseas promotion of Jamaica and the Reggae Boyz team in the wake of the last World Cup football tournament. Another discussant said, "Dem [the government] fi build workshop and get yout' off the street fi learn a skill."

In summary, the discussion underscored the following:

- The links that youth in inner cities make between unemployment, lack of skills training, jobs and crime.
- Attitudes to tourism were mainly positive with these inner-city youth seeing opportunities that could be utilized to offer specialized services to the

tourism sector. They favoured such inputs as theatre in education productions, community education using skits, and tour guide services to groups that wanted to know more about life in the ghetto.

While the majority of members live in harsh social conditions, their attitudes, training and knowledge are not necessarily typical of many other ghetto youth, many of whom have not enjoyed their level of exposure through organizational involvement. Their positive responses do reflect the fact that with training and support, positive attitudes to tourists and to the industry can be generated among people who are deprived of proper social economic and domestic amenities. The positive responses of these inner-city youth contrast sharply with the responses (discussed earlier) from ghetto youths in Flankers, near Montego Bay.

CHAPTER 4

Report on Community Meetings

A total of five community or school-based meetings were held to explore in a more free-flowing manner citizen attitudes to tourism and other related issues. Table 4.1 sets out the location and composition of these meetings. 'Community' in this context is regarded as either people living or working in a common geographical area, or alternatively people sharing a community of interest. These meetings provided a forum for larger more expansive discussions on issues and attitudes to tourism.

Rio Bueno – Trelawny

The small fishing community of Rio Bueno is located on the main north coast road between Discovery Bay and Duncans. It is part of Trelawny, a parish with a limited but growing involvement in the tourism industry. The Rio Bueno community offers a range of tourism products and services including an art gallery, restaurants, fruit vending, wood carving and other craft items on stalls along the main road.

Table 4.1: Community Meetings

Community	Parish	# Participants
Rio Bueno	Trelawny	9
Association of Women's Organizations of Jamaica (AWOJA)	Kingston	20
Negril All-Age Senior Class	Westmoreland	29
Bluefields People's Community Association (BPCA)	Westmoreland	12
Portmore Community	St Catherine	30

Source: Dunn and Dunn (Survey data)

The community meeting included nine residents: five men and four women. Although the meeting was not organized under the aegis of a community association, word spread about the topic to be discussed and several persons volunteered to participate, as they seemed anxious to register their views. A Rastafarian craft vendor who had been operating the main craft stall in the area for the last eight years, played the most active role in the discussions, with two of the women, both unemployed, also contributing strongly. Most of the other participants were fishermen, farmers or fruit vendors.

The women expressed great concern about the lack of opportunity for work in the community and concern for the future of their children. A few residents had obtained work at the Braco Village Resort but they felt that the majority of the employees there were from outside of the Rio Bueno/Braco area.

The owner of the main craft stall felt strongly that it was Jamaicans like himself, an artistic Rasta man, who reflected the authentic base of the tourism industry. He said it was the tens of thousands of ordinary Jamaicans who provided a real taste of the country for visitors. He argued that they were the ones who offered unique natural products and warm hospitality to the tourists: "We are the people who really represent the Jamaican tourism product and who are most photographed and displayed on JTB and hotel posters." Despite this reality of using such people to sell the industry abroad, he said, the Jamaica Tourist Board and government made little effort to directly assist these producers – who were vital to the success of the industry.

He noted that the emphasis in terms of resource allocation was in the direction of accommodation, but he wanted it to be widely known that "HOTELS ARE NOT THE MAIN REASONS WHY PEOPLE COME TO JAMAICA". He said good hotels exist in the countries where most of the visitors are coming from and, like beaches, they are all over the world. What makes the Jamaican industry special was not hotels but "the hospitality of the Jamaican people and the fresh, unique products like music, culture and other services offered by Jamaicans".

He also said the people who needed the most attitude change were the tourism planners. He felt that they neglected these creative Jamaicans and were "sucking up" to what he called the "money gods in the big hotels". Other participants who seemed to share his opinions strongly, wildly applauded him for these views.

The fishermen and food vendors in the meeting complained that like the craft vendors, they got little help in producing for the industry, although they regarded themselves as working in a tourist area.

Association of Women's Organizations of Jamaica (AWOJA)

The meeting with AWOJA took place at the headquarters of Sistren Theatre Collective in Kingston. Twenty women, mostly drawn from the professional and non-governmental sector attended the meeting. The women ranged in age from late teens to over fifty, all with a shared community of interest in the development of women and in the social and economic advancement of the country. The discussion started with identification of the benefits and drawbacks of the industry. Considerable uniformity was noted among participants about these issues, as presented in the following summary:

Benefits from tourism

Tourism is a very important industry for the country, with important spin-offs in employment and foreign exchange earnings. It is recognized, however, that a considerable portion of the foreign exchange earnings from tourism either leaves the country or does not enter our economy at all. We have hosted generations of visitors. More recently, the emphasis on community and ecotourism has spelled an increase in visitors from Europe, in particular. In addition, several people returned after tertiary training abroad in an effort to become involved in the sector.

Problems

Some speakers expressed the view that the great majority of ordinary Jamaican traders and vendors were marginalized in terms of direct contact with tourists and in terms of economic benefits. They felt that popular resentment was building up at the effect of the all-inclusive concept, and there were already signs that such feelings could erupt in the form of roadblocks and other protests. Except in immediate resort areas, the average Jamaican did not see tourism as directly benefiting him or her.

Some members of the group felt that television and newspaper advertisements still tended to reinforce stereotypes of the white/wealthy tourist being wooed by the bright smiles of the servant/black hotel staff and street urchins. Some examples may be found within overseas promotional programmes such as the "Come back to Jamaica" campaign advertisements. While there were exceptions, persistence of the old stereotypes excluded our national achievements in health, education, the arts and sport.

One AWOJA member cited TV and newspaper coverage of US spring-breakers who were engaged in non-stop drinking and "lewd" dancing. This she said formed another and equally negative side of depicting Jamaica as a place where "anything goes" and where one is encouraged to let loose. The attitude appears to be "we drunk them from they arrive til they leave". She also felt that such portrayals continued to send wrong signals to local and foreign teenagers, in particular. Another speaker pointed out that Barbados was host to some 40,000 spring-breakers – compared to our 20,000 – but the tone and thrust of their product did not appear to be as "salacious" in content as that of Jamaica.

Prostitution and economic deprivation

Several participants suggested that prostitution from tourism would continue to increase as long as Jamaica's economy remained poor. Prevailing economic conditions hold out little hope for people to be gainfully employed as well as to develop the required sense of hope and dignity. In addition, it was felt that the images and ideas expressed above had created a mindset that our country offered mainly "sea, sand, sex and ganja" which were seen as powerful adjuncts of the so-called sex trade. Some members of AWOJA argued that these sexually titillating images went to the heart of our self-worth: "Are we still being bought and sold?" one member asked. She also queried: "Why no images of our professionals, educators, sports personalities? Why are we invariably seen as smiling market women or Rasta children, tagging along beside well dressed white people?"

Treatment of black people in resorts

It was noted that there were not enough voices calling on the sector to encourage black tourists to come to Jamaica. Another participant detailed the hostile reception recently received by her and members of her party at a certain hotel on the North Coast, where they were given inferior treatment, compared to white visitors. She felt that black Jamaicans still suffered humiliation at the hands of hotel staff who clearly behaved as if 'black' is synonymous with 'harasser'. To be black and perceived as a working class person compounded this hostile treatment. The importance of culturally appropriate training, not just technical skills, was also emphasized.

Several members were strongly opposed to any attempt to prevent access by Jamaicans to the best beaches and attractions. Others expressed concern that in future, children may only hear about certain locations, as they could be barred from entering them.

Recommendations

The main recommendations advocated by participants included:
Education programmes: The need for radical change in attitudes towards Jamaicans vacationing in Jamaican resorts must start with a re-education of the persons at the top of the industry, as it was felt that it was at that level in particular that a 'house-slave' mentality towards white foreigners appeared to be most ingrained. It must first be taught and accepted by Jamaicans – before it can be displayed – that our offering to visitors must be a people's cultural heritage, not just 'sea, sand and sex'. Re-education in schools must be the linchpin of government policy. It was felt that only a tiny handful of the population understood that promotion of the tourism product was best done by those who experienced the real hospitality of our people first-hand.

Training workers in the industry: Training of all tourism workers, including managers, was necessary. These stakeholders should be informed that a 'tourist' was not synonymous with 'white/affluent'. Asians, especially the Japanese, have increasingly swollen the numbers of visitors to our shores; the trend has been no different among black Americans and the British who have been coming here to reconnect with their roots. Some of these have also come out of an interest in being in a country where people such as themselves are in the majority and in control of government. Participants felt that these groups must be acknowledged and welcomed.

Promote community tourism: Community tourism must be the drawing card: we must invite our visitors to see us as we live and work. It was noted that the international trend was for the authentic and the natural and that these features must be emphasized, particularly heritage and ecotourism. What we lacked in geographical size could be compensated for in diversity of attractions. However, these attractions must be based on our realization that we are an intelligent, creative and dignified people.

Promote culture and heritage tourism: Increase promotion of Jamaica as *the* place for cultural/heritage studies. It was generally agreed that if for none other of its achievements and distinctions, Jamaica was recognized and has become world-famous for its reggae music and its reggae star, Bob Marley. More summer classes could therefore be offered to visitors using our music as the gateway to many other cultural/historical journeys. Participants also pointed out that there was much to be gained from promoting our herbal remedies.

Priority sectors: There was consensus that tourism should *not* be our primary economic focus, because the country could not be sustained by any single sector but needed a mix of sectors that would create backward and forward linkages. However, without doubt, it was felt that we needed to tackle and resolve persistent problems relating to health, education and infrastructure, as benefits to be enjoyed by Jamaicans *first*, and *then* extended to the visitors. It was stressed that the provision of better roads and services was necessary not because of tourism but because it was critical to the sustained and orderly growth and development of the country.

Children – Grade 6, Negril All-Age School

The researchers conducted a class discussion with pupils of Grade 6 at the Negril All-Age School. The participants, numbering 29, were all children in the 10-to-14 age range. The objective here was to elicit from the young students an indication of both their knowledge levels and their emerging attitudes about tourism and their community. As one of the faster-growing tourism resort areas, Negril provided a good context for this class discussion. Many of these children had previously participated in JTB's 'Hello Tourist' project. Their recollections and reflections could therefore be expected to be more informed and thoughtful. For the same reason, however, their level of awareness would not be typical of children their age in most other schools.

The children were asked who they consider a tourist to be. Two sets of answers emerged from the early stages of the class discussion. They argued that a tourist was a person who came from overseas to spend holidays. Probed further, those who supported this view said the tourists could be of any race or colour. The other position was that a tourist did not have to come from abroad but was simply a person of any race or colour taking a trip for relaxation, pleasure or health reasons. We then took a show of hands for agreement with one or the other position. Less than one-third of the class (8) agreed with the first position about a tourist being a foreigner visiting a country. A large majority (21) agreed that arrival from overseas was not a necessary criterion for defining a tourist. A child of the latter group illustrated this by saying that if he went to Ocho Rios or Kingston for a break with his parents he would be a tourist there. A girl holding the opposite view created some laughter, however, when she told him that he would be just a 'dry land' tourist. She said while he might regard himself as a tourist in Kingston nobody else would. Most members of the class eventually agreed, however, that a tourist need not come from abroad.

The children were asked to show hands indicating whether they felt they would be treated better or worse as Jamaican tourists in a Jamaican hotel. Twenty members of the class said they would be treated the same as a foreign tourist, six said they would be treated worse and three said that they were not sure. None of the children felt they would be treated better. However, it was significant that most of the children expected to be treated in the same way as a foreign visitor.

Regarding the economic impact of tourism, the dominant view was that everybody benefited from the industry, but that some people benefited more. The latter, they noted, were owners of hotels, planes, banks and big shops. They felt craft vendors, 'carvers', taxi drivers and restaurant owners also benefited to some extent. Among those whom they named as not benefiting much from tourism were teachers, students, library employees and policemen.

Regarding the messages they had heard about tourism on the media and in school, these Negril children recited the tag line "Don't Harass the Tourists" and some said they had been told to treat tourists with love and respect. One child indicated that she was told that people should not try to rob the tourists and that everybody should help to give them directions about where to find places.

Recommendations from the children about how to improve the industry included:

- Plant more flowers in the town
- Prevent pollution of the sea water
- Give people more work
- Put up posters about Jamaica

In addition, the children felt that they could assist with many of these activities.

Bluefields People's Community Association (BPCA)/ Westmoreland

The Bluefields community is located on the south coast, an emerging region for Jamaica's tourism product. The BPCA is a civic development agency consisting of citizens from a range of neighbouring villages including Belmont, Brighton and Whitehouse. There were also participants from Negril, Savanna-la-Mar and Race Course in Clarendon.

The Association focused on integrated community development, with a strong emphasis on environmental issues and rural communication. It housed the embryonic Bluefields Community Radio station (now defunct) and other information and documentation resources. The meeting at BPCA took place with twelve participants from the community. These included five women, ranging in age from 19 to 55 years and seven men in the 25 to 50 age group. Most of the participants were farmers, small business people and social workers, with some indirectly dependent on tourism for a living.

The majority of tourists seen by these residents were regarded as low to middle income visitors from many countries or areas, and included Jamaicans on holiday from overseas. "Many of them come here on credit, and have to face a big debt when they return home," one participant said. Another observed that many back-packers were on hiking trips across the area and some of them reckoned on staying with local families. One member of the group felt strongly that while there was a place for those in the lower end of the tourism market, this was the segment most involved in the drug and prostitution business. "Most of them come to crash," he said. Other participants pointed out that it was the visitors who brought some income into many rural areas and that not all of them were seeking or selling drugs.

A more mature woman in the group said that the quality of local accommodation available to these visitors was quite poor. If rural homes and sanitary facilities could be improved with government loans or direct assistance, many more ordinary householders would be able to earn a living from accommodating tourists in their own homes. Most participants agreed with this, but noted that local people should have contact with a mix of visitor types, including those at the upper end of the market who tended to frequent the large hotel properties.

One officer of the BPCA drew attention to the need for more community information and education about tourism, especially on the South Coast where the industry was just beginning to develop. He saw an important opportunity for good attitudes to be fostered before the area became more developed and affected by bad attitudes.

A young participant was concerned about making better arrangements to deal with the environmental impact of tourism in the fragile ecosystem of the South Coast, including the beaches, mangroves and rivers in the area. It was suggested that there should be a direct levy on visitors for development of the environment and broader measures in place to ensure that more of the money earned in tourism was spent in tourism related areas.

Commenting on the quality of products marketed to tourists by craft vendors, members of the group complained that there was too much duplication of items. There needed to be more innovation and variety if sales to tourists were to really grow.

Portmore citizens and community leaders

Portmore is regarded as one of the largest residential communities in the English-speaking Caribbean, housing more than 250,000 residents. Located in the parish of St Catherine, it borders both the old capital, Spanish Town and the current capital city, Kingston. The area consists of a large number of neighbouring housing developments occupied by mainly middle and lower middle income families, with a high density of professionals.

The community meeting in Portmore took place in the amphitheatre of the Portmore Mall. It was attended by a group of about thirty residents. In addition, the entire community meeting was transmitted live on one of Portmore's major subscriber television services, Jamaica Amalgamated Cable Systems (JACS) Limited. The discussion lasted for just over an hour, with several telephone calls being received and responded to during the live programme.

Leading the 'studio audience' were eight panelists drawn from different sectors of the community. These included the chairman of the Portmore Joint Citizens Association (PJCA), a senior teacher at one of the major secondary schools in the area, a hotel employee resident in Portmore, the manager of a seafood restaurant in the community, the public education officer of a major utility company servicing the area, an economist from the community, a media manager and a local media specialist who did the initial introduction of the participants to the audience.

All the participants ascribed great importance to the tourism industry, and the economist indicated its contribution and central importance to the country's macroeconomic development. The tourism employee offered a definition of a tourist as a visitor from overseas. Others on the panel immediately challenged him and argued that if employees approached the industry as a service sector for foreigners only, it was not surprising that Jamaicans often received such poor service in hotels. The hotel employee felt the need to correct his initial definition.

The teacher who wore a second hat as guidance counsellor said the country's high school curriculum itself defined a tourist as a visitor from overseas. Corrections at the level of the Ministry of Education were essential. These would foster accurate knowledge and appropriate attitudes to Jamaican vacationers.

Most participants and callers felt that the industry contributed most to the wealthy sector of society. There was also the view that it contributed most to people in certain parishes and resort areas. There was strong support for a new vision of an industry as encompassing the entire country. The call among members of the panel was for every region or parish to examine what they could offer as a complement to the existing stock of attractions. Inland trails, music, art, theatre productions, local foods, ecotourism and historical/cultural sites were among the suggestions offered.

The chairman of the Portmore Joint Citizens Association pointed to the fact that the area already hosted a large number of resident Jamaicans and overseas visitors to the Hellshire beaches. There were many restaurants and guesthouses on the Port Henderson Road. The vacant and deteriorating former Forum Hotel was cited as a potential location for a new beginning – such as a cultural centre and educational or training space. A caller into the programme identified the prospect of jobs emerging from a hospitality industry in Portmore, to which the economist and the public utility officer agreed.

Another caller was concerned about the ecological and environmental effect on Portmore of an expanded visitor industry, given the already congested roadways and limited public amenities. Other members of the panel responded sympathetically to this view, and insisted that the country and areas like Portmore must be developed primarily for its residents who could then extend hospitality to visitors. A member of the audience said that they might not have the luxury of doing one or the other and that the facilities of the area would have to undergo accelerated development for both local residents and visiting patrons.

Recommendations to promote tourism in and around Portmore included:

- Establish trails to explore wildlife and exotic plants in the Hellshire Hills.
- Promote seafood and watersports in the bays and beaches of the area.
- Organize tours of agricultural properties and old sugar cane plantations in the Bernard Lodge and surrounding estates.
- Promote horse racing at Caymanas Park.
- Develop and extend use of the Jamworld grounds as a concert and exhibition venue.
- Integrate marketing of neighbouring attractions including sites in Portmore, Kingston, Port Royal and historic Spanish Town.

Communication Messages

- The JTB and the Jamaica Information Service (JIS) could collaborate more to strengthen public education about the importance of the industry. This kind of promotion needed to be on-going in both traditional resort areas and non-traditional tourism locations. Every effort should be made to involve the citizens, their associations and the business community in the area.

- Increase involvement of the JTB in the schools, providing resource persons and fostering more tourism clubs.
- Place tourism messages on cinema screens in the community, on local cable television in the form of sponsored programmes on tourism issues.
- Use more posters, billboards and mainstream media messages.

The televised event was well received and on return visits to the cable television company, the researchers were told of continuing discussions in the community about the programme and its ideas. The Portmore Citizens' Association had decided to place the issue of tourism on its agenda for further discussion. In addition, comments from businesses such as local seafood restaurants and neighbouring farms indicated a renewed vision for their Portmore enterprises.

Public education alternatives

This initiative of getting a successful community meeting via cable as well as assembling a panel of key leaders and residents from an area provided a model of both participatory research and public education methods.

CHAPTER **5**

Reflections and
Recommendations

The data emerging from these discussions would suggest a need for fundamental restructuring not only of industry relations but of the industry itself. The overwhelming view emerging is that the industry benefits large investors (and to some extent government) to the detriment of small entrepreneurs and ordinary people in the industry. There was also the strong perception that even in areas where resort properties were located communities did not benefit sufficiently from the industry. In addition, there was a firm view that it was the role of the government to mediate the flow of these benefits towards a more national and equitable relationship with communities.

Restructured media and educational campaigns could not adequately address these problems and would be futile unless there was fundamental industry restructuring in line with many of these legitimate concerns. At the same time, there was insufficient acknowledgement in public expressions that individual initiative was crucial to developing a 'people-based industry'. There tended to be high expectations of government intervention to rectify imbalances. There is doubtless a role for government in this. However, if more people adopted the approach of the young farmer in Windsor Castle, Portland, much more could be achieved at the personal and community levels: Instead of complaining or producing exactly the same product as his neighbour, this farmer marked out a spectacular mountain trail, organized a Neighbourhood Watch to help secure the area, and so developed a popular environmental attraction. He reported that he had already secured bookings for two years in advance for certain hotels that took advantage of this added attraction.

This episode also contains important lessons for hotel operators and all-inclusive properties. While these large operators had expended promotional resources to attract large groups of visitors, restricting these tourists to activities within their resort compounds was not a sustainable route towards development of the local tourism product. It is true that there is a high level of concern about the security of our visitors. However, more could be done to train and employ many of the local residents as tour guides and security personnel. Already many tourists have complained about a lack of contact with local people and cultures; at the same time there is an increasing emphasis globally in the holiday package that explores people's lifestyles and the indigenous flora and fauna. Sooner or later, more and more visitors, particularly Europeans and Asians, will lose interest in and decline the return visits to luxurious beachfront properties, the swimming pools, mass produced foods and the activities of 'entertainment coordinators', for the very same reason.

As the craft vendor from the Rio Bueno area of Trelawny noted, hotels and beaches are available in most resorts anywhere in the world. The distinguishing 'value added' components were to be found in the flavour of the local community and the attitudes of the people. It would serve the wider industry well if closer links were established between the large hoteliers and the neighbouring communities and attractions. The alternative would be to risk a simmering hostility already evident in a section of the urban youth reaching to boiling point.

If the strongly expressed views of the young men in the Flankers area of Montego Bay are anything to go by, then it is urgent that the ghetto communities adjoining most resort areas be factored into the future planning of the industry. They themselves must begin to organize for their training and educational needs. Even as government's Tourism Master Plan envisages a doubling of stopover arrivals and a tripling of cruise passengers in the next ten years, so too could the number of unemployed and disaffected persons in these areas multiply. Unless more training and employment opportunities are created in neighbouring communities, the persistent problems of harassment and criminal activity will continue to increase.

These include the creative public education programmes that form part of the tourism development strategy. Several groups see citizen contact with foreign tourists as a key feature to be encouraged. Many visitors want to know first hand about local attractions and about people's lives. The increasing tendency to regard this contact as tourist harassment will need to be reviewed. Clearly, there are criminals who aim to exploit and even harm visitors if given a chance. But this risk has to be better managed to ensure that most community youths are not treated as criminals for responding to the enquiries or curiosity of a foreign visitor.

The findings from the focus group discussions and community meetings complement the survey data in concluding that there are serious issues of racism within the resorts and the wider industry. Black Jamaicans and other visiting black people report that they receive distinctly inferior treatment in many hotels. Discussants in one of the corporate area community meetings pointed out that this problem might well originate in the attitudes of senior managers and owners of some of these properties. It was observed too that this attitude was often mirrored in the behaviour of frontline employees, who also brought their own measure of bias.

The discussions among the school children in Negril and the panelists in Portmore suggested that part of the problem had to do with perceptions of who was a tourist. It was disclosed that in sections of the official school curriculum and in popular usage, a 'true' tourist was regarded as a visitor from overseas. Many also equated this with a white foreigner on holiday. While historical patterns in the development of the industry may have reinforced these views, the need for re-gearing of attitudes through re-definition and public education is very evident. The ambivalence occurs even at the highest institutional levels in the industry. For example the *1999 Annual Travel Statistics*, a publication of the JTB, defines visitors as "any person visiting a country other than the one in which he/she normally resides", and a tourist as "a visitor staying at least 24 hours in the country".

This official attitude no doubt gets transmitted to all levels of the industry and can inadvertently result in negative treatment of Jamaicans vacationing in their own country. It is therefore reassuring to note that the 2001 edition of the *Draft Tourism Master Plan* published by the Ministry of Tourism offers a revised definition in line with the concerns expressed by many of our respondents. That document defines 'tourist' as "anyone who travels away from home (country, parish, town) for a stay of one or more nights for holidays, visits to friends or relatives, business, conferences or any other similar purpose". This broader and more inclusive approach will lend recognition to those hitherto derisively referred to as 'dry land tourists'. The new definition also brings the contemporary foreign visitor more in line with most of their local vacationing counterparts in being seen as mostly 'ordinary working people who have saved their money for a holiday'.

At the same time, the fact that such persons bring money into the Jamaican economy is not lost on most of our respondents. For 1999 alone, the JTB estimated income from foreign travel to be J$51.2 billion or US$1.2 billion. People recognize as well that at a different level visitors also bring both friendship and possible negative values with them. Many lasting relationships of friendship have been built between Jamaicans and visitors of all types, resulting in multiple repeat visits, adoption of the country or a particular resort as second home. Many personal life-partners have found each other, as romantically immortalized in the novel and film *How Stella Got Her Groove Back*. In our survey, friendships ranked second only to the financial gains brought by the industry. However, negative values are third in line. The responses reflect people's recognition that nothing really comes free. They see a downside in terms of possible illegal drugs and prostitution that are regarded as negative factors but are nonetheless part of the traded goods and services in the industry.

Issues of poor roads and other infrastructure continue to be a problem for residents, industry workers and visitors alike. The need for better housing for tourism employees was also highlighted in many responses. While these remained urgent concerns in the most recent interviews, improvements in public transportation and in the incidence of crime in resort communities were also reported.

The assembled data make the case for a thorough and on-going public education campaign about the importance of the industry to Jamaica's economy and future development. It is important for the campaign to stress that even communities with no tourists benefit from tourism dollars to finance many social facilities and services. Such a campaign strategy also has to show people in resort communities how the income from the industry is being ploughed back into infrastructure development and better services. The conventional approach of spending promotional budgets entirely in the overseas markets has been modified, with the result that some resources are being spent on local advertising and public education. Such an approach will need to be expanded in response to the growing potential for local tourists and in response to evidence of misconceptions within and about the industry.

Summary of main findings

Perceptions of the personal, community and national benefits from tourism among those interviewed and solutions proposed

Most people (86.4 percent) regarded tourism as very important to Jamaica. More than half (56 percent) said they were either involved or had family members involved in the industry. This included nearly a third (30 percent) who said they depended directly or indirectly on tourism for a living. An additional 26 percent said that they had family who worked in the industry.

Most people felt that tourism was of no benefit to their community. More than a third (36 percent) felt that the impact was moderate. Only a quarter (26 percent) felt that the community benefited a lot or reasonably well from tourism. General perceptions of 'who benefits most' and 'who benefits least' were clear-cut. There was a very strong view that it was the 'big man' who benefited most and the 'small man' who benefited least. The 'big man' was most consistently symbolized as owners of all-inclusive hotels, travel and airline operators and in-bond merchants. The most popular images of the 'small man' were as local taxi operators, craft vendors, higglers, farmers, hotel workers and operators of local villas and guest houses.

Improving benefits from tourism

In rank order, the most important changes proposed to bring more benefits to the Jamaican people and economy were: using more local foods, improving security in tourist areas, improving roads, promoting rural and environmental tourism, improving training for people in tourism, using fewer imported products (not only food), and promoting more cultural and heritage tourism. These perceptions are consistent with the view that many communities are not benefiting sufficiently from the industry and the perception that it is the 'big man' who benefits most.

Perceptions of who a tourist is

The dominant perceptions of tourists were that they were "visitors from overseas" (46.3 percent). Another 27.3 percent felt they were "people of all races" and 19.2 percent said they were "white foreigners". The latter view-point indicates that there are still Jamaicans who associate tourists with Caucasians from abroad. Only 7.2 percent said they were "guests in a resort hotel", which could suggest that many people did not acknowledge local persons as potential tourists.

Perceptions of the financial status of tourists

More than half of the survey respondents (54.3 percent) saw tourists who came to Jamaica as "ordinary working people who had saved their money for a holiday". Almost a third (31.3 percent) saw tourists as "well-off people with reasonable amounts of money to spend". Less than 10 percent saw them as "rich people with lots of money". The remaining 4.8 percent indicated "other" reasons. The most frequent view within this group was that Jamaica's tourists were a combination of the three categories.

Perceptions of the influence of tourists on life in Jamaica

Analysis of the frequency of responses to this question showed that *money, building friendship* and *negative values* were the three most important ways Jamaicans saw the tourism industry making an impact on the country.

Perceptions of the treatment of Jamaicans on vacation

There was a widespread perception that Jamaicans were treated worse than overseas visitors, although there was a core who felt that Jamaicans were treated the same. Almost half of those interviewed (53.5 percent) were of the view that Jamaicans received worse treatment than overseas visitors, while almost one-third (32.4 percent) felt they were treated the same.

Perceptions of problems and proposed solutions

The three most important problems identified were crime and violence (59.3 percent), bad roads (38.5 percent), and visitor harassment (29.1 percent).

The main solutions proposed in rank order were more community education, better street lighting, and stiffer penalties for harassers as well as more police and resort patrols. The least popular solution was introducing large numbers of soldiers into resort communities.

Perceptions of priority sectors for economic development

Almost half of the respondents (48 percent) felt that tourism should be the *second* most important sector (38 percent) after agriculture to ensure the future development of the country. In rank order, the remaining priority sectors were manufacturing (30 percent), information technology (23 percent), and bauxite (19 percent).

Messages and media sources on tourism

Seventy percent of those interviewed remembered seeing or hearing advertisements in Jamaica about tourism. Nearly all of them (68 percent) were able to recall where they had seen or heard the advertisements. Cable television, local TV and local radio stations were the most popular sources. The study found that over half of those interviewed watched more cable than local TV.

Recommendations

The findings strongly suggest that improved communication strategies and more effective messages will not by themselves improve attitudes to tourism or tourists, or build a stronger stakeholder base for tourism to flourish. Rather, a national effort is needed to create an enabling environment that will allow the industry to survive, grow and maximize its tremendous potential.

Poverty eradication, infrastructure improvements (roads, low-income housing, street lights) and urban redevelopment initiatives are considered critical to the success of tourism. Education, skill training and employment creation must complement existing efforts to improve the tourism product.

The creation of a friendly and welcoming environment for tourists also requires that a combination of educational and security measures be used to tackle the problem of harassment.

In light of the findings and analysis, the following recommendations were made for action by the appropriate agencies, mainly the Office of the Cabinet, the Ministry of Tourism and the Jamaica Tourist Board.

Restructure the industry and promote community tourism

- Address perceptions of alienation and inequitable distribution of industry benefits by restructuring the industry to expand community and small business involvement in tourism.
- Encourage more active partnerships between all-inclusive hotels and local businesses to expose hotel guests to more Jamaican attractions in the community.
- Inform public and private sector groups of niche market opportunities such as executive buses/shuttles between urban centres (for example, Kingston) and resort areas (for example, Ocho Rios); build houses to meet the needs of workers in resort areas.
- Encourage partnerships between government, private sector and non-governmental organizations (NGOs) to increase the variety and distribution of attractions beyond traditional tourist resorts. Market those that meet industry standards to all visitors.
- Investigate and address the concerns of local transport providers who complained about monopolies and other injustices in the transportation of cruise ship and other visitors to sites and attractions.
- Develop communication programmes targeted at local audiences to create and sustain a positive public attitude to tourism and to highlight its overall benefits to the country. The messages should be clear, simple and gender specific.
- Encourage all-inclusive hotels to link the activities of their guests to local events and community attractions and to highlight their contribution to employment and local development.

Expand communication and public education

- Develop a strategic marketing programme aimed at policy makers in the Cabinet, in strategic government ministries and in tourism agencies. This would seek to encourage a more integrated, multi-sectoral approach to the development of tourism as a long-term sustainable industry.

- Create messages that clarify 'who is a tourist' to reinforce dominant perceptions of tourists as visitors from overseas and to change the remaining perceptions of them as essentially 'white people'. Show images of visitors from overseas *and* images of Jamaicans, on holiday.
- Reinforce perceptions of tourists as ordinary people with images of them working to save for a holiday to their favourite Jamaican destination.
- Interview Jamaicans on vacation to explain why they holiday here. Include statistics and graphics on the number of Jamaicans who spend holidays in Jamaica.
- Develop messages for the electronic and print media that build on the strongly held view that in addition to money, tourism creates friendships between people of different countries.
- Develop anti-drug messages targeted at communities in and around tourist resorts as well as at incoming visitors. These should reinforce existing reminders about Jamaica's drug enforcement laws.
- Improve security information to tourists to enable them to protect themselves.
- Develop communication programmes to encourage and promote diversification and to inform visitors and the country about new products, services and attractions.
- Use more innovative non-formal approaches for public education. For example, more face-to-face interactions/community discussions; more use of theatre in education (TIE). Other ideas could include: a tourism drama festival; selling tourism as a theme for national festival competitions; commissioning a major play or pantomime on tourism for staging in communities throughout the island.
- Decrease local and overseas use of well-worn and stereotypical images of Jamaica and Jamaicans, and replace them with more modern images and uplifting representations. Recognize that cable television now brings overseas promotional campaigns into local homes.
- Develop and expand strategic alliances with NGOs, churches, community groups, schools and youth organizations. Spend more of the tourism advertising dollar in Jamaica. Promote local resorts at all levels – advertise tourism services, properties and attractions.
- Channel more messages through cable, local TV and local radio. Use communication channels that are widely accessible and popular. Messages

for local audiences should use clear simple language that Jamaican audiences can appreciate.

- Expand JTB programmes that provide opportunities for more Jamaicans to meet tourists.
- Expand educational programmes through schools including the full integration of tourism into the national schools curriculum.

Visitor Harassment in Negril Jamaica

A Community Case Study

CHAPTER **6**

Negril

Problems in Paradise

Negril – mecca of the sun-seeker, site of a world famous seven-mile beach-front, venue of exotic resort nightlife. The laid-back atmosphere with breath-taking sunsets is legendary. This rustic, back-to-nature retreat regularly showcases Jamaica's culture through throbbing reggae rhythms at planned dancehall sessions and at other cultural events. Paradise indeed for tourists in search of relaxation and the roots of Jamaica's culture! But is this once idyllic resort headed in the direction of 'paradise lost'?

One of Negril's most prized possessions as a tourist destination, is its environmental appeal and the welcoming attitude of residents and workers. Threats to the environment have been a recurring concern over the years and the spectre of 'visitor harassment' looms large over the future of the resort. The people who live and work in Negril are the first line of protection of the natural and social environment around them. But the Negril resort community is also a national resource requiring keen attention and focus by policy makers if it is to develop into a sustainable, long-term base for the tourism industry. This study is a contribution to that process of reflection and policy analysis, which must precede and accompany action.

Definitions

The *Concise Oxford Dictionary* (1990) defines the word 'harass' as 'to trouble and annoy continually or repeatedly, or make repeated attacks on an enemy or opponent'. Most Jamaicans would not regard visitors to the island as enemies or opponents and relatively few visitors are physically attacked. However when several persons 'trouble and annoy visitors repeatedly' it constitutes harassment.

An inclusive and useful definition of the term 'tourist' has recently been adopted by Jamaica's Ministry of Tourism as outlined in the summary of the "Draft Ten-Year Master Plan for Sustainable Tourism Development" (mimeo, circa 2001). The Plan defines a tourist as 'anyone who travels away from home (country, parish, town) for a stay of one or more nights for holidays, visits to friends or relatives, business, conferences or any other similar purpose'. This is the meaning which will be employed as a definition of tourists in our references here.

Trail of visitor harassment

Interviews and observations in Negril revealed a trail of harassment with several layers that crossed social and economic barriers. For visitors from overseas, it often starts at the airport and continues in various forms until they leave the island.

At the airport, the attitudes and behaviour of some immigration and customs officers as well as baggage handlers constitute explicit forms of harassment. Their approach wears out already tired travellers. Inadequate information and preparation for overseas visitor arrivals in Jamaica also set a framework for harassment. For example, paucity of information signs on the cost of baggage handling and ground transportation at the airport often forces the overseas visitor to make unguided enquiries leading sometimes to misinformation and overcharging. Visitors who do not acquire this information before arrival are not adequately informed about or given guidelines on arrival on tipping, transportation costs, exchange rates and the general cost of living in case they want to explore local shops and businesses. Some visitors also need advice on how to handle the problem of harassment or how to deal with local persons who approach them offering unsolicited goods or services.

Transportation is an essential service as visitors try to get from the airport to their hotel as well as around resort and neighbouring communities. Some taxi operators were identified as being a major source of harassment. Competition to carry tourists is stiff and jostling for passengers or reports of overcharging are quite common. As in the main resort areas, many hotels in Negril provide transportation between the airport and their properties. A two-tiered taxi system offers both luxurious airport service and more modest local taxis rides. Fierce competition between the two can be stressful and confusing for overseas tourists, especially if they have not made prior arrangements.

Once in Negril, the trail of harassment often continues at the hotel or guesthouse, where tour company representatives may 'strongly encourage' the visitor to pay for non-refundable packaged tours during their orientation session. Subsequent exposure to other tour options and entertainment choices may leave the visitor without the flexibility of a refund.

Once on the streets, harassment intensifies as visitors try to explore their surroundings, purchase goods and services, hire transportation, or visit the various attractions on offer. Even while walking or relaxing on the beach, enjoying the scenery or purchasing souvenirs, visitors are likely to be approached by several persons offering a range of goods and services. Others may be trailed by persistent persons who calculate that they will 'let off a smalls' (a small amount of money) to be rid of them.

Local visitors travelling from Kingston are sometimes similarly exposed to harassment en route to Negril. For example, shrimp vendors in Middle Quarters (St Elizabeth) and fish and bammy vendors in Whitehouse (Westmoreland) often descend on vehicles in droves in search of sales. Once in Negril, depending on their colour or social background, they too may have a similar experience to tourists from overseas.

Early tourism in Negril

A brief history and overview of the resort provides a context for this case study on visitor harassment. Hayle and Associates (2000) in their carrying capacity study, provide a succinct history of Negril dating back to the eighteenth century. Their study notes that since the 1960s, the area has been transformed from a fishing village to a major tourist resort community, capitalizing on the spectacular and picturesque 12 kilometres of white sand beaches. The first hotel established in 1965 catered to "wealthy retired Europeans and Americans" (p. 67). In the early 1970s, Negril became a haven for the hippie sub-culture of North America. The establishment of resort hotels like Hedonism II and the all-inclusive Sandals in more recent years has contributed to a change in the character of Negril.

Consistent with its focus on tourism as the main economic activity, Negril's land use, facilities and other resources have been skewed in favour of visitors. An analysis of the *Negril Development Plan* (1994) produced by the Town Planning Department shows that more than one-half of the land available (53 percent) was in use as resort facilities. This is in sharp contrast to the 15.2 percent of land used for residential purposes and the 4.8 percent used by squatters. Commercial space occupies 3 percent, the airstrip 2 percent, open space occupies 0.3 percent and public assembly areas 0.6 percent. Only 20.9 percent of the remaining land space is vacant (Hayle and Associates 2000: 68).

Formal and informal commercial activities have been established on the three main roads that run through the resort and converge at the Negril roundabout. There are basic facilities such as an all-age school, health centre, police station, fire station, library and a few churches. The quality and scale of services for local residents have not kept pace with the growing population, however, and have been disproportionate to the investments for hotels. This unequal development and allocation of resources result in an imbalance in facilities for visitors and local residents which we argue is one of the factors contributing to harassment.

Negril attracts two or three main types of visitors with varying income levels. These reflect the dual character of the resort, which is organized to accommodate both luxury guests and the more informal low budget holiday-makers. The latter group includes United States college students on Spring Break. In the Long Bay beach area on the Norman Manley highway, the number of resort hotels, water sport facilities and craft shops has expanded. On the West End Road, towards the Lighthouse and the 'Cliff' there has also been an increase in the number of small cottages, guest houses, villas, restaurants, bars and craft centres.

These profiles of Negril's 'West End' and that of Norman Manley Boulevard reflect differing land ownership patterns. The government and the Urban Development Corporation primarily owned land in the Long Bay Beach area adjoining the Boulevard. Most of the land in the West End has been family lands which local residents have used to capitalize on the tourism market. Hayle and Associates (2000) provide a valuable analysis of the positive and negative impact of tourism on family land in Negril. They suggest that the government should provide training to family members who invest their land in tourism. This should address both the problems and benefits of the industry as well as ensure that high standards are consistently maintained (Hayle and Associates 2000: 56–59).

As Jamaica's third largest tourist resort community, Negril has experienced enviable economic growth since the early 1970s. In 1993 the estimated population of this resort town was 19,911. McHardy (1998) notes in the "Master Plan for Sustainable Tourism in Negril" that investments in Negril have facilitated the growth of the tourist industry in Westmoreland. As a result, an estimated 90 percent of Negril's population work directly or indirectly in tourism (see Boxill 2000: 26).

The character of community life is quite different from the other tourist towns of Montego Bay and Ocho Rios. It tends to have a more 'laid back' atmosphere. Many visitors interviewed said that they "return to re-live fond memories and re-establish old acquaintances". This has significant marketing implications for the sector, suggesting that if the visitor's first experience is positive, he or she will return and spread the good news, which will then have a multiplier effect as they encourage other visitors to come. The strong marketing message is that *people promote tourism*.

This state of harmony and friendship often found in Negril is ideally what a resort aims to achieve. The question of how long this area will remain as a relaxed resort town largely depends on whether or not the problems of visitor harassment and environmental degradation can be solved.

Visitor harassment, a major challenge for the tourism industry, takes various forms and crosses all social barriers. Prostitution, drug peddling, crime, violence and high prices are among the problems giving rise to deep concerns on the part of tourism authorities, hoteliers, some tourists, workers, and the wider public. Harassment threatens the sense of peace and security that visitors need in order to relax and enjoy their holiday, and is therefore a major deterrent to their return to Jamaica and to resorts such as Negril.

Most hoteliers are Jamaicans. In our survey, over 90 percent of them agreed that visitor harassment was a major problem. These hotel operators were using several security measures to reduce harassment on their properties. Their perceptions of the problem varied. A few recognized that "not all tourists were upset by certain types of harassment". Others agreed that the pestering of tourists occurred at several levels and in various forms, involving a wide range of people. There was also the recognition that big business operators who paid touts to inveigle tourists into their premises were also involved in harassment.

While most visitors had experienced harassment and saw it as a major deterrent to enjoying their holiday, not all were put off by it. Their views are explored in more depth later in the study and are compared with those of vendors in Negril. Vendors who operated in established locations who had been exposed to training by tourism agencies, acknowledged that harassment was both widespread and detrimental to business. Their views contrasted widely with those of many informal traders, hustlers, taxi drivers and some residents of low-income communities, who did not see the problem as an important issue.

This latter group did not view their persistent approaches to visitors as harassment. Rather, they felt that they had a right to earn a living by offering goods and services to visitors in the same way that large establishments did. In their view, selling to visitors allowed the 'small man' to get a share of the tourist dollar which was controlled by the 'big man' (all-inclusive and large hotels). In summary they were just 'getting a piece of the pie' and trying to distribute the benefits of tourism more evenly between ordinary Jamaicans and the 'big man'. Imbalance in the distribution of benefits from tourism therefore emerged as one of the main factors contributing to visitor harassment.

A 1971 IDB-funded study conducted by the University of the West Indies (UWI) noted that it was "doubtful whether incomes earned from tourist expenditures percolate throughout these economies" (Boxill 2000). Another study by the Centre for Population Community and Social Change (1999) makes a similar reference to Ocho Rios (Hayle and Associates 2000). The Report on the Task Force on Tourism (RTFT) (1995) also underscored the importance of linking tourism with other industries, especially within the services sector.

Harassment has an economic cost to tourism. It contributes to a downturn of visitor arrivals – a consequence not unique to Negril but which has serious implications for foreign exchange earnings for the national economy. This also applies to the Negril community where the industry is the major source of survival for the majority of residents. Boxill (2000) reports that 90 percent of the total population of Negril is estimated to work directly or indirectly with the tourist industry.

Negril's visitor harassment problems cannot be viewed in isolation from the socioeconomic reality of the town and the surrounding communities. This resort area has become the entertainment and income-generating hub of the network of communities in the western extremity of the island. In the parish of Westmoreland, where 81 percent of the population live in rural areas, urban Negril bears the burden of being the most developed centre for miles around. Recent studies show that Negril has 2 percent of Westmoreland's population and 8 percent of its retail establishments (Boxill 2000). High unemployment in Westmoreland and surrounding parishes is a push factor while the employment opportunities offered by tourism in Negril serve as a pull factor. The level of unemployment or economic inactivity among men in the parish was 30 percent or just less than twice the national average. The situation was, however, dismal for women in Westmoreland. Preliminary results of the 1991 census indicated that in comparison to the men 70 percent of the women were economically inactive – an unemployment rate twice that of men in the parish and over four times the national average of 16 percent.

Many neighbourhoods in Westmoreland are satellite communities of Negril, in terms of employment and accommodation for workers. They also provide some agricultural and other supplies. Some of these outlying communities, such as Cave Valley, Mount Airy, Sheffield, Grange Hill, Little London and Green Island suffer severe social problems of unemployment, poor housing, bad road conditions and inadequate water and other social amenities. They exist in sharp contrast to the exotic accommodation of Negril's hotels. For many of these households, basic services such as water, electricity and sanitary conveniences are luxuries. At the last national census, figures for Westmoreland indicated that some 6 percent of private households in the parish were without toilet facilities and 79 percent used pit latrines. Over 7 percent used water from untreated springs, rivers and public tanks and only 13 percent of private dwellings had access to piped water. Close to 30 percent of Westmoreland households relied on public standpipes. More than half of the households (53 percent) used wood or charcoal for cooking and 46 percent used kerosene lamps for lighting at nights (STATIN 1991 Census for Westmoreland, published 1994). The emerging profile of poverty indicates a sharp contrast between the standard of living of visitors and that of many local people.

Visitor harassment must also be analysed against the background of low-income and squatter communities coexisting with a tourist resort in a relatively small area. As previously noted, the boom in tourism has been a pull factor which has expanded the population in and around Negril. When census data for Westmoreland are compared for the periods 1970–82 and 1982–1991, they show a net loss in population for the parish as a whole, but show an increase in the population in the Negril area of the parish. This suggests that many people in Westmoreland have moved to other parishes, and significant numbers have migrated to Negril.

Unequal development in infrastructure and facilities for visitors and local residents in and around Negril is also an issue. Significant efforts have been made over the years to upgrade the infrastructure for tourists, expanding the number and range of hotels and villas. Over the past thirty years, construction activities in Negril have resulted in the addition of some 130 rooms annually. Boxill (2000: 31) notes that between 1991 and 1997 approximately 273 housing solutions were completed in Negril by the formal sector. However, this was insufficient to address the problem of both residential and commercial squatting which has accompanied the boom in Negril's tourism industry. The pattern of migration from other communities indicates a greater movement of females than males to tourist areas. Residential squatting was "as high as 6.2 percent of the built-up area and has been unplanned, with most of it being concentrated on government lands such as Whitehall, which has 5,000 residents, the majority of whom are from Hanover" (Boxill 2000: 31).

Environmental problems also emerged as major factors discouraging tourists in both our 1994 Negril study and the follow-up study in 2001. One of these is squatting, which is a major problem threatening the very survival of Negril. Several related problems including pollution of the South Negril River, unsafe and unsightly commercial and residential structures on the banks of the river, and damage to the social and natural environment have been highlighted. McHardy (1998: 41, cited in Boxill 2000) notes that more than 60 percent of this land is used solely for commercial purposes, 3 percent for residential and 7 percent for mixed commercial/residential purposes. Some 43 percent of the businesses provide food, 7 percent are garage/repair shops and the rest are hair salons, clothing, laundry, hardware and auto marine stores. Approximately 70 percent of the respondents in that survey had no access to toilet facilities and of the 30 percent who had, about half had pit latrines and a quarter had water closets; 25 percent had neither of the above types. All of the sewage disposal systems used absorption pits rather than holding tanks. Wash water from the kitchens, the laundry, restaurants and hair salons was allowed to drain into the morass.

These practices damage the ecosystem in the long term, pollute the water, damage the reefs and reduce the overall physical attractiveness of the area. The negative environmental impact of squatting must be addressed as a matter of urgency if Negril is to remain a viable tourist resort. The Negril Watershed has been designated as the Negril Environmental Protection Area including the morass, marine ecosystems and moist forests of the Fish River Hills. The Negril Marine Park was declared as part of the national system of parks and protected areas in 1998. Research findings by the Negril Coral Reef Preservation Society (1997) indicated that coral cover in Negril has eroded from 80 percent coverage in 1970 to between 5 and 10 percent coverage in 1997. Loss of coral has had a negative impact on fish stocks and reefs, and contributed to erosion of the shoreline, among other negative effects.

Stiff competition between various social and economic groups striving for the tourist dollar sets the stage for pressure on visitors. There are conflicts between the large hoteliers and squatters, hustlers and craft vendors. Craft vendors in turn blame itinerant vendors and others who come into the area to do business in illegal drugs and prostitution. Both are considered lucrative businesses, further complicating the conflicts between these groups. The introduction of all-inclusive properties has improved security for visitors but has also sharpened the social conflicts as access to visitors in more limited. When these visitors do venture out in tour buses, the time is limited for purchases and some orderly locations with local vendors are bypassed.

Other social conditions in the resort area contribute to the problem of harassment. These include poor educational services, with only one school in Negril (the Negril All-Age School), limited health services, poor recreational facilities for residents, high unemployment and poverty levels, poor water supply and sewerage facilities, inadequate solid waste disposal and poor road access, particularly to residential communities. Failure to attend to these problems will result in low morale of employees, poor self-esteem by residents and a reduction in the level of return visits by loyal tourists.

Spring Break in Negril

Among the developments fueling debate on the nature and future of the Jamaican tourist industry has been the growth of the college student tourism market during the annual pre-Easter holiday period. In 2000 arrivals on Spring Break between late February and early April peaked at 33,000, generating revenues of US$22.6 million. While income levels dipped by about US$5 million in 2001, the expenditure of just over US$17 million from 25,000 Spring Breakers would have boosted stopover arrivals in the specific resort areas of Negril, Montego Bay and Ocho Rios. In Negril, where our research team collected data during March 2001, the young Americans numbered 15,000, making Negril the country's most popular Spring Break resort area. These 'Spring Breakers', as they are called, displayed specific characteristics and made their own peculiar demands in service delivery in the resort. They did not want the all-inclusive packages, preferring low cost hotels, which allowed contact with local people and events. This new group of visitors is different from the traditional visitors to Negril who "return to relive fond memories". Some do, but research is needed on this new development to determine patterns of their arrival among other factors. Their arrival has also been a pull factor as local people try to cash in on the opportunities to offer services and goods to young people seeking musical entertainment, sex, drugs and alcohol which they would be prohibited from having in their own country because of age restrictions.

Hoteliers appear to have mixed feelings about this new group of visitors. While welcoming their patronage, some have been cautious because of their past experiences with them. Some hotels frequented by the Spring Breakers reported only minor instances of property damage and a high incidence of minor mishaps. According to the Negril police, the traditional problems of excessive alcohol consumption and sexually explicit conduct on stage and in-group activities were restricted over the last few years. Increased police warnings as well as plain-clothes and uniformed police surveillance continued to limit and control illegal activities.

Some hoteliers complained of a limited spread in the benefits from this market, and local vendors noted the distinctly low levels of expenditure by some of these visitors. They showed a distinct preference for large group activities at venues organizing a range of musical and on-stage entertainment. At some events, beer and rum are served free as a means of getting the visitors accustomed to local brands, which are also marketed overseas. This represented a recognition that the Spring Breakers market goes beyond the immediate returns from current expenditure. Both the hotel and other product marketers saw the longer term benefit in creating new customers who would return as fully established adults, bringing their families and other acquaintances with higher disposable incomes.

Objectives and Research Methods

Concerns of industry officials about tourist harassment, poor work attitudes of industry workers and environmental issues were some of the factors leading to the commissioning of the original study of Negril in 1994. The Tourism Action Plan Ltd (TAP) commissioned the research in association with the Jamaica Tourist Board and the Negril Resort Board. Using the same survey instruments, the researchers conducted a smaller follow-up study in March 2001 to determine if any changes had occurred since 1994. Most of the key findings remain unchanged.

In this publication, we update and renew our data analysis to provide quantitative and qualitative baseline data on the Negril resort community. The objective is to facilitate a more informed understanding of the dynamics of tourism in this resort community and to deepen understanding of people's attitudes to visitors and to the environment. The results have already helped to guide the development of policies and programmes of the Jamaica Tourist Board and the Negril Resort Board and continue to do so.

To better understand the problem of visitor harassment, both studies focused on workers, vendors, tourists and hotel operators. In each case, we sought to:

- identify the attitudes to tourists and to the problem of harassment, noting any changes between 1994 and 2001;
- identify tourists' perceptions of harassment;
- develop a socioeconomic profile of Negril with details on the major sources of employment;
- identify skills training needs for workers and vendors;
- identify appropriate public education and training strategies to change the attitudes and behaviour of workers and vendors in the industry as well as the public.

The study collected both quantitative and qualitative data, using a combination of research methods. These included questionnaire surveys; documentary reviews (including police records); observation of life in and around Negril; focus group discussions and interviews with hoteliers and industry specialists.

A total of 250 respondents participated in the 1994 and 2001 surveys, in which systematic samples yielded an average response rate of 98 percent. The quantitative findings are presented in both the narrative text and in tables starting in chapter 8. Some of the tables presented in these chapters indicate comparative data relating to the surveys of 1994 and 2001. All other tables relate to the 1994 survey.

Interviewer-administered questionnaires were developed for workers and vendors and a third questionnaire for tourists. For purposes of the study, Negril was divided into three main geographical areas: the West End Road, the Norman Manley Boulevard and the Savannah-la-Mar/Negril Road. The sample of workers and tourists was drawn from randomly selected small, medium, and large businesses, hotels and micro-businesses in these three areas. The sample of vendors was drawn from the Negril Vendors' Plaza; Sunshine Village Complex; Rutland Point Craft Park; Adrija Plaza; Summerset Village Craft Plaza; Negril Craft Park; the West End Road; the Norman Manley Boulevard; and the Savannah-la-Mar/Negril Road.

In the chapter which follows, the reports of in-depth interviews are reproduced and analysed to form the main body of the qualitative findings.

CHAPTER 7

Talking Visitor Harassment

The Negril Notebook

The mini case studies in this section provide profiles of some of the more controversial and visible forms of contact between locals and visitors. It is within this zone that the issue of harassment arises. Although these instances do not cover the wide range of persons engaged in this activity, they do provide some insight into the attitudes of workers and vendors to visitors, as well as indications of the perceptions of the visitors themselves.

The professional pimp

"I Am Addicted to Tourists . . ."

'Michael Andrews' (not his real name) was spotted in animated conversation with a white male tourist in the food court of the Singles Plaza, Negril. The tourist left the restaurant via the stairs and rear exit to the West End Road. Andrews followed closely behind, talking to the tourist who seemed anxious to get rid of him. The visitor headed down the West End Road, towards the

Negril roundabout, and he followed. Both came to a stop on the sidewalk, about ten yards from the exit, and the tourist went into his wallet and handed him a note. He accepted it, shook the hand of the tourist dramatically, and the two went in opposite directions. The tourist continued walking briskly towards the Negril town centre and Andrews turned back and walked up the road to enter the food court from the rear of the plaza.

As a Jamaican visitor to Negril, the interviewer engaged Andrews in light conversation and eventually established the following background information and profile.

Michael Andrews was clean and tidily dressed, with a neat haircut and a pleasant approachable countenance. However, his clothes showed signs of wear and he was physically quite slim. He was 30 years old, but appeared much older. He gave his address as Westland Mountain, a community off the West End Road, where he lived with his common law wife and four children, ages ranging from 7 to 12 years. He was very articulate and intelligent, with a ready sense of humour. He was originally from Mandeville but reported that he had been in Negril for fourteen years. He was the second to last child in a family of 9 children (8 boys and 1 girl). All of them went to "secondary school," including Andrews who considered himself the "bad egg". His father did manual work at Alcan and his mother was a housewife. He came to Negril at first "to look work".

Once Andrews became convinced that the interviewer was not from the Police Department, he relaxed, opened up and told his story. He admitted to being a self-appointed "tourist assistant" and "tour guide". Andrews confessed that he was "addicted to tourists" (his words) and felt compelled to offer them something as he knows that he is likely to get some money in return. He regarded himself as being among the best at his job in the Negril area, and did not "work" anywhere else or do any other job. As a result of approaching and offering services to tourists, he had been arrested many, many times and, after convictions, had served six terms in prison. The offences included soliciting, offering services without a tourist guide's licence and possession of drugs. He claimed to be well known to the police by his proper name as well as by his many aliases, which he recited.

His first offence was being caught with 25 pieces of crack, which he had cooked-up from powdered cocaine, using baking powder. He said he was first taught to prepare and use hard drugs by a tourist, and knew that many of them came down mainly for access to ganja and other drugs. Andrews maintained that, despite his activities, he was not a thief and was only trying to make a living. He also distanced himself from the "rent-a-dread" types, whom he said were mainly after money for "nasty kind of sex with white people". He considered himself more of a tourist guide and supplier. He said, for example, that the tourist he was talking to in the plaza and on the sidewalk "asked him for aloe vera as a natural skin treatment for sunburn". He (Andrews) asked for a hundred Jamaican dollars, but "afterwards the man gave me J$500". However, based on the observation of the interviewer, this may have been the price the tourist had to pay to get rid of Andrews, but according to him, "The tourist did not want any change."

Andrews reported that he could make a few hundred or up to five thousand Jamaican dollars a day, depending on "the season" and the "kind of currency" he obtained. Despite the risks, he saw no other jobs with this kind of return for a skill, which came to him naturally. He was not interested in farming, although he recognized that he was getting to the age when he would have to start thinking about "something else", and expressed the hope that "Maybe you can help me."

Andrews explained that there were about 25 expert tourist touts in Negril, with the rest being less skilled, less regular or just starting up. However, nearly a half of the most skilled touts are in prison. "Only about ten of the best one dem lef pon de street right now." He said some younger ones were coming up to take the place of those in prison. (During the conversation, Andrews handed out two crisp $50 notes to a youth about 10 years old, who was hanging about the plaza and said to the interviewer: "Him a try, yuh nuh.")

Andrews said that it was common knowledge that "some a de police dem deeply involve inna di drugs business", and that he knew this "as a fact".

In summary, Andrews was a professional male pimp, offering services and drugs to tourists. He had migrated to Negril in search of work and had a family to support. Despite several arrests and prison terms he persisted in his profession, motivated by the level of income his work sometimes offered, his need to support himself and his family and his unwillingness to seek alternative forms of work that offered less income. Tourists had reportedly introduced him to hard drugs (crack/cocaine), and his interaction with them had convinced him that many come for drugs which was one of the goods and services he could supply. He however had his standards and would not engage in "nasty sex", which some were seeking; nor would he steal. He was proud of his "profession", considering himself one of the best in the business. Andrews also gave some insight into the population of persons engaged in his "profession", which was relatively small, but no doubt had a significant impact on Negril because of the community's size. As half of his colleagues were in prison, it appeared that the strategy was to keep the numbers on the street to a manageable number. In all likelihood, they too would return to pimping, regarding a prison term as a mere 'occupational hazard'.

Industry officials therefore face the challenge of finding appropriate interventions to change the attitude and behaviour of persons like Andrews and his associates, or a structure to modify their behaviour and set limits on their activities. This was important as at 30 years old, he was at the peak of his career and recognized the need to find an alternative source of income. Training Andrews to be a proper tour guide, providing him with an income that will compensate for his other activities and helping him recognize how his illegal activities impact on the industry may take years. It would address his need to be recognized and to respect the personal standards of morality he has set for himself in not being a 'rent-a-dread' or 'selling nasty sex'. This highlights the need for a harassers' rehabilitation programme in some form or the other.

Currency trader and part-time pimp

"I can make a good money . . ."

'David Johnson' (not his real name) was 17 years old. His main work in the previous year involved getting customers for foreign currency traders but he did other jobs. He was known by a nickname on the plaza. He once worked as an assistant in a farm store, but said he was overworked, got little pay and had no free time. He came to Negril from a neighbouring district to help earn some money to support his mother and other relatives. His father died years ago and he was the main source of income for the family.

David hung out in the car park of the main plaza near the Negril roundabout, together with 6–8 regular illegal currency traders. Between 10–12 other hustlers also acted as agents for large currency traders or as small scale traders themselves. David was not very well dressed, striking a sharp contrast with many of the other currency traders on the plaza, who were doing the same thing, but were very sharply dressed. David was a poor youth, just trying to break into the business. At 17 years old, he was a relative newcomer and estimated the average age of the other more established agents as being early to mid twenties. They worked at soliciting tourists or local customers to change US dollars or sterling to local money or vice versa. Like most of the other young agents, David had little if any US dollars of his own. When he found customers, David tried to negotiate a rate and either took or directed the customer to the parked car of the bigger fish', who then completed the deal seated in the cars or at some discreet point in the plaza. With bigger deals, clients were transported to other locations for the transaction. The real dealers were established personalities in the Negril community. Approximately four or five bigger dealers operated from that plaza complex. Their ages ranged from 27 to 45 years. Some were from outside Negril (Petersfield, Savannah-la-Mar) and others were from the area. They operated in flashy cars and were reportedly respected among the agents and other youth around the area.

In return for bringing customers, David was paid about J$2,000 for a day's work. Sometimes he made nothing if business was slow and supplemented his income by guiding tourists to the craft village across the roundabout. This was especially profitable on days when "Sandals bring plenty tourists and let them out of the bus to go to the duty free shops". He reported that most tourists asked for directions to the craft shops and he followed them, and got a tip at the end. He did not leave them until he was given a tip, which varied between US$5, $10 or $20 dollars depending on what they felt like giving him.

However, he could also make extra money in the dollar trade for his bosses on the plaza if he negotiated a slightly lower rate with the customer and he then claimed the difference. This boosted his earnings and he reported that he could make up to J$2,000 for a good day's work, but this is not very often for him as a newcomer. Others made more, and also traded their own money. David said that some taxi-drivers on the plaza also dealt in currency.

David also doubled as a drug pusher and agent for prostitutes. The latter was his night job as his regular day job as a self-employed foreign currency trader was proving slow at that time. "Some tourists or even locals might want some coke, so me can go and get it fi dem. If I go buy it fi dem, a charge a different price from what I get it for . . . an' ah keep the difference. So ah can make a good money." Similarly, David can direct tourists to clubs where they can get prostitutes, and he collects money from the women the following day. There were two main points in the town where the prostitutes could be easily found. He could earn an extra J$5,000 a week from this kind of work.

David wanted to get into craft work or learn a trade, but did not see his way and was doing the hustling in the meantime.

In summary, David was engaged in various types of harassment. Like Andrews, he had migrated to Negril seeking work to support his family. Frustration with a low-paying job and poor working conditions led him to become involved in currency trading and he had devised various ways of securing an income from transactions and the trade. In addition, he worked as a pimp for prostitutes, earning income from these sex workers as well as tourists seeking sexual services. In addition, David doubled as a 'tour guide' and drug pedlar, always seeking income for services requested or offered.

At age 17, David was still legally a child, but had assumed the adult responsibility of providing for his family. Unable to pursue his career goal of becoming a craft worker or a tradesman, he engaged in activities that enabled him to survive.

Addressing the problem of harassment perpetrated by young men like David would require not only providing support for his training, but also ensuring adequate support for his family. Between the 1994 and 2001 studies, the introduction of the cambio system had somewhat eroded the livelihood of young men like David, who have had to explore other strategies for earning an income – some of which no doubt result in visitor harassment.

The mindset of some visitors also needs to be examined. Most white men in their home country would not follow a black man they did not know to a car in a parking lot. Those who would are more likely than not to be interested in transacting business that is illegal. There are risks associated with this behaviour as much in Negril as in New York. It must therefore be recognized that some visitors are willing to and do engage in illegal acts, which makes them open to exploitation by locals. Guests disregarding normal security precautions also fuel the harassment trade, and these regulations should be part of the orientation and public education programme aimed at overseas visitors in particular.

The tour guide

"Tony: West End tour guide"

"I tell tourists where to go if they want a whore" or any other entertainment.

'Tony Blake' was a well-dressed young man, very cagey and unwilling to talk about his activities. He reported that he visited Negril once or twice a week, but he knew the area quite well. According to him, he helped tourists to find their way around. He said he has "no other work to do but to make some money". He showed tourists from the West End, the best parts of the beach, "where to go if they want a whore" or any other entertainment.

He was a graduate of a prominent High School in Manchester and was from a large family. He made contact with tourists anywhere, including on the beach, on the West End Road or in the plazas.

In summary, Tony, a secondary school graduate, was a migrant worker who visited Negril, lured by the opportunities of providing services to visitors who were unfamiliar with the area and needed 'advice' and 'direction' to get around. Like David, he provided a range of services as 'tour guide' or as pimp identifying persons who could provide sexual services for tourists. Like his colleagues, Tony was young and his education indicated that he had the capacity to develop his skills beyond his current income-generating activities.

Industry officials face the challenge of identifying and facilitating education and training alternatives and convincing young men like Tony to pursue these alternatives instead of harassing tourists.

Have dreadlocks – will travel

Offering "Good strong sex"

'Desmond Wilkinson', (not his real name) is a 32-year-old dreadlocks from Negril, living in a lane off the West End Road. He had been a craft maker in the market for over 12 years, and would sometimes take the tourists out to the clubs. One year ago he met Mary, a 45-year-old Canadian visiting Negril from Ohio. She was a successful herbalist and physiotherapist, whom he called a doctor. According to Desmond, Mary had many clients, a plaza of her own and over 300 acres of land overseas. She fell in love with him, and would seek him out every time she visited Negril. He was not serious about her but she was determined. One day he decided to think seriously about her. She invited him to the United States where they later got married. She took his surname and everything was official. He was now quite settled with her abroad, but visited his relatives in Negril regularly. When in the country, he rented a car to get around and he and his wife had just bought some land in Negril.

Desmond said many people asked him what was in it for the woman. All he could say is that many of the single or even married women tourists come to Negril to experience "good strong sex". This attraction is based on their idea that a black man can give them more than a white man can. He was now quite contented and regretted that he had not made the move earlier.

Desmond's story illustrates another motivation and source of contact between visitors and local residents. Though not unique to Negril, its laid-back, relaxed atmosphere is seductive and sex is among the many services on offer. There is no suggestion, however, that this is the main attraction. Nevertheless, some visitors from abroad come for a sexual experience to live out a fantasy associated with the racist stereotype of sensual, overly-sexed black males and females. This myth provides an opportunity for local men and women to provide sexual services. This contact also offers the possibility of travelling abroad or migrating. The phenomenon of the *rent-a-dread*, is another dimension of this stereotype, describing the trend for black males to grow dreads or wear dreadlocks wigs, to fulfil this image. The mane of dreadlocks adds to the mystique and power associated with the strong black male who can provide "good strong sex".

Sex for sale: The tale of two female prostitutes

'Sandra' and 'Norma' (not their real names) aged 27 years and 18 years respectively worked as a team in Negril, selling sex services to local and foreign males, especially at nights. In the afternoon they worked as waitresses – one in a bar and the other in a hotel. Both were from Hayes in Clarendon and came to Negril to fend for themselves. Both had dependents: Sandra had a five-year-old child while Norma had parents who depended on her for support. Norma was the youngest of nine children and three of her five brothers were police officers in Kingston but did not help the family much. She however felt that if she got into trouble her brothers could "arrange something" although she admitted that they did not know what she did for a living. Both of Sandra's parents were dead but as the eldest of five children, she had to provide for her younger siblings as well as her own child.

Both women frequented the tourist towns of Montego Bay and Ocho Rios and had started coming to Negril because they felt they had become too well known by the public and the police, and the traditional resort areas were becoming too crowded. They found Negril "a bit boring" but decided to remain to "cool out" nevertheless.

Sandra had started working as a prostitute from age 19 years, and therefore had been in the business for eight years. Her preference was for "di white man dem because dem treat yuh better and hardly ever run off without paying". She said some even adopt her as a friend "for the whole of their visit" and take her out to "nice places". According to Sandra, "They still have to pay a minimum of US$100 per night – or maybe more." She disliked the Italians because they "wanted to have sex for free" or "fi pay little or nothing". She added, "Nuff a di whore dem in Negril get old now and most of di young one dem don't want to work in dem own town." Sandra felt she could go full-time working as a waitress or bartender. She however did not want to work as a dressmaker, which was the trade she had started to learn as a young girl.

Norma was just starting out and did not know what she wanted to do for the future. She did not want to "go into the go-go dancing side of things" because according to her, "mi too shy". She relied on Sandra for support in approaching or talking to men and they travelled together for security at nights.

It is not accidental that only two of the case studies profile women. As the records of police arrests show, most of the persons arrested for related offences are men. Like Desmond, Sandra and Norma use their body as a commodity, selling sexual services, to meet a demand among Negril's tourist population. Also like Desmond, they sometimes develop relationships with their clients over a succession of visits, but "it's still strictly business", as they have to earn an income to support their families. Both have also migrated to Negril from other areas and are also migrant workers in the sex tourism industry.

Norma presents one type of challenge to industry managers, while Sandra presents another. Norma is very young, unsure of herself and not yet integrated and comfortable in her role as a sex worker. Training, the opportunity to work as a waitress full-time, or in some other occupation of a non-sexual nature, may provide her with legal choices to earn a living in order to support herself and her family.

Sandra is intelligent, older, more experienced and has a good head for business. She takes the decisions to rotate locations when things get too hot in one tourist destination. She is also focused, practical and able to separate friendship from business with her clients. Finding legal activities that provide a comparable income will be more challenging but not impossible.

Synopsis

These case studies provided excellent sources of feedback on the attitudes, origins, motivations, needs and operational methods of some local citizens who are in direct contact with visitors or who may be regarded as engaging in tourist harassment. They were all originally from outside of Negril, and came to the area looking for work. Most were young and unemployed. Most of them were males. Many of the other pedlars and itinerant vendors interviewed conformed to this profile of the young male tout. The beginner was young, unemployed, had some secondary education and was attracted to Negril as a place to hustle. Had they been reached in school or in the initial stages of involvement on the street or beaches, the chances would have been quite high of re-directing their energies into alternative occupations. The fact that Andrews indicated that there are many new youths just starting out as hustlers, suggests that industry managers have the opportunity to stem the flow into this type of 'work'. At the same time, these pedlars and so-called unofficial tour guides are responding to a felt need among the visitors to Negril, otherwise they would not find these activities viable and rewarding. The picture emerging from several interviews is that they are exploiting the need of tourists to talk with and get assistance from local citizens.

Prostitution is another form of harassment. Females dominate in this market, but males are also involved as 'rent-a-dreads' and 'beach boys' providing both heterosexual and homosexual sex to visitors. While these studies did not focus explicitly on the sex tourism market, other studies have examined the issues extensively in Jamaica (Jamaica Ministry of Health 1996; Campbell et al. 1999; Dunn 2000) and in the wider Caribbean (Kempadoo 1994; Davidson 1996; Davidson and Taylor 1996a; Davidson and Taylor 1996b; Kempadoo 1999; Kempadoo 2001). In Negril, the sex tourism market has been formalised by the provision of some resort properties that focus on providing an environment for exotic and erotic sex holidays. Street prostitutes harass visitors to buy their services. Dunn (2000) in an ILO study on child prostitution in Jamaica, found that some of the female and male prostitutes in Negril were under the age of 18 and therefore classified as minors. Managing the market for sex tourism is another challenge for the country's tourism industry planners, health workers and educators. The implications for national development need to be carefully examined and addressed as a matter of urgency. The Ministry of Health is already recognizing and developing interventions for the male and female sex workers in this subsector.

As previously noted, the existence of male and female street touts, suggested the need to reexamine and broaden the tourist guide scheme for Negril. Training could be provided to the regular male guides, to enable them to become truly professional. With training and inputs from the police, the hoteliers and the schools the problem of would-be harassment could be reduced. This would give the authorities greater control of the situation and would enlist the support of the current 'offenders' in helping to ensure 'good practice'. The focus would be on giving these youth opportunities to develop a legitimate stake in the success of the industry. Ongoing monitoring and public education would help to ensure the maintenance of minimum standards.

Many of the young men interviewed had become involved in harassment by offering tour guide services which often led them to seek narcotic drugs required by and for their clients. Some did pimping for prostitutes on the side or sold currency. The approach to addressing this problem could include promoting a strong anti-drug campaign in primary and secondary schools and extending this into the wider community, using unconventional techniques. A second strategy would be targeting the large drug and currency dealers in a joint intervention involving senior police and military personnel. Law enforcement would complement public and youth education against drug peddling and should be done in collaboration with national programmes to reduce the demand for drugs in communities.

Andrews' attitude to his 'work' suggests that he never seriously contemplated the negative effects of his actions on tourism, but mainly saw these as opportunities to provide services, even if unwanted, for financial gain. Despite having repeatedly suffered imprisonment, he was prepared to persist as this was the best way he knew of making a living. He was however "getting on in age", having done this 'work' for over a decade, and was at a point where he was open to other options that could assist him in supporting his family. This represented an opportunity to re-direct him on a different course as, clearly, imprisonment and enforcement were not effective deterrents. Many of his cohorts were in prison and the same observations could apply to some of them. While out of prison, they played a role, as we have seen, in fostering pre-teens and other youths into touting activities in order to 'help out'. It is clear that some strategies need to be directed at this group. Training and employment for these tour guides faces the challenge of providing comparable income to that provided from illegal activities. Education and training programmes in prisons are also needed to change attitudes and behaviour patterns of this captive audience.

While recognising that many tourists come to Negril to enjoy the beauty of the physical surroundings, the reality is that some visitors come for the services offered through direct contact with local residents. Good customer service results in visitors who return. Bad experiences such as harassment result in negative publicity and a reduction in visitor arrivals. Most vendors interviewed were aware that the problems of tourist harassment, crime, illegal drugs and high prices were major deterrents to the return of some visitors. Visitor harassment also emerged as the dominant deterrent in the more recent study suggesting that it is still a major problem seven years later. The research also showed that in rank order, high prices, crime and violence, garbage and poor water quality were main deterrents and therefore remain important issues for the attention of industry managers. Against this background, public education programmes should continue making the link between harassment and a decline in repeat visitors, and harassment as the reason why more visitors gravitate towards all-inclusive hotels. Public education messages should also help local residents to understand that if they play their role in re-creating Negril's historical character as a safe, laid-back resort, they will benefit financially as visitors will return – and send their friends.

Public education messages targeted at local businesses and vendors should also link high prices with poor sales. Other messages should stress that a clean environment makes Negril 'nice'. These must however be accompanied by improved sanitation and garbage collection services, upgrading in water quality and close collaboration among environmental and tourism agencies. Policies and programmes must seek to bring HEART Trust/NTA programmes to Negril to train young people. These, together with poverty reduction and employment programmes at both a national level and in outlying villages, will hopefully reduce crime, violence and harassment.

8

Craft Vendors in Negril

Profiles and Perceptions

Profile of vendors

This section of the report provides a background profile of two groups of
vendors in Negril as well as their attitudes and perceptions of visitors. The
first group is comprised of vendors operating in established designated
locations and the second consists of itinerant vendors who operate on the
streets and beaches of Negril. Analysis of these two groups and their perceptions of visitors can improve our understanding of the factors that contribute
to visitor harassment and can inform the development of training and public
education programmes and strategies to reduce the problem.

Established vendors

Established vendors operated in one of several plazas in and around Negril
that were designated for vending. These sites were: the Vendors' Plaza and
Sunshine Plaza on the West End, Rutland Point and the Negril Craft Village

on the Norman Manley Boulevard and Adrija Plaza near the Negril round-about. Unofficial craft sites also operated on the streets of Negril, as well as on the main roads to Summerset Village, Cotton Tree and Savannah-la-Mar.

The 1994 study identified a population of 253 vendors in the five main established locations in Negril. Of these, 55 were located in the Negril Vendors' Plaza on the West End Road, 103 in the Negril Craft Village, 54 were at Rutland Point, 41 in the Adrija Plaza and an unknown quantity on the streets of Negril. There were also an additional 30 vendors on a waiting list to get accommodation in the Vendors' Plaza at the time of the study. This sample of vendors was drawn from the main established craft sites in Negril.

Demographic profile

Sex

Women dominated the sector. More than half of these vendors were women who accounted for 55.4 percent of the sample, while men accounted for 44.6 percent. This overall picture compared favourably with data from the Negril Vendors' Plaza, which showed that 69 percent of occupants were female, compared to 31 percent male. Observations of vending sites also confirmed that women were largely responsible for marketing and vending. Perhaps it was attractive to women as it provided scope for them to combine their domestic duties with earning a living as self-employed micro-entrepreneurs. Some types of craft items could be produced on the same site at which they were selling, thereby combining their 'factory' and 'marketing' outlets. Craft vending also provided an opportunity for the women to own and control their own assets, however modest and irregular the income it provided. This information can be useful in designing training and other support programmes for vendors. The 2001 study confirmed this prevailing gender balance and activities profile.

Age

Vendors between 25 and 49 years accounted for 80 percent of the sample. Almost one-half (46.4 percent) of the vendors interviewed were in the age group 25–34, and 33.9 percent were between 35 and 49 years. These statistics have implications for training as few younger people (under 25 years) were choosing vending as a career. In general school children had a negative attitude to vending. This was confirmed in the focus group discussions with school leavers at the Negril All-Age School, who looked down on street or market vending and only saw it as an option if there was nothing better to do. These findings on attitudes, age and gender have implications for the future sustainability and character of the local craft industry. Interventions will have to make it more attractive to young people through diversification and a different approach to skill training and micro-business credit.

Education

Craft vendors tend to have a basic education to the level of an all-age school (Table 8.1). The study showed that they were more likely to have secondary or all-age school education (48 percent) or primary school education (30.4 percent). Very few (9 percent) had been to high school. In light of these findings positive consideration should be given to continuing education. Short courses on specific topics should be a component of any training programme for this target group. The content and methods must always take account of the literacy and numeracy levels of the specific target group.

Table 8.1: Education Level of Vendors

Education Level	%
Primary	30.4
Technical/Vocational	7.1
Secondary/All-Age	48.2
Other including High	14.3
Total	100

Source: Dunn and Dunn (Survey data)

Marital Status

Consistent with national trends, over one-half of the vendors in the sample were single (54 percent); another 21 percent were married and 21 percent were in visiting relationships, while the remaining 4 percent were either widowed, divorced or separated. More than half of the vendors were single women with children. If the national average is used as a guide, approximately one-third of these women are likely to be single heads of household, living on a very low income. These are important factors to be considered for both the training and public education programmes. While the scope of our research undertaking did not allow us to explore the actual age of the children, we were able to ascertain the number of dependents of each vendor.

Dependents

Sixty-six percent of the vendors had adults to support. Of these 39 percent had at least one, while 18 percent had between two or three children to support. The majority of vendors (84 percent) also had dependent children with 48 percent of these having between two and three children to support. These findings imply that the income earned by most vendors supports at least three additional persons. The emerging picture of poverty also has implications for visitor harassment. Although further research would be needed to ascertain the actual situation, these findings point to a low standard of living for the children in these households, which in turn adversely affects their access to basic amenities and services such as food, shelter, education and health. It also presents a scenario that invites child labour and child prostitution. While the 2001 tourism study in Negril did not make any link between the children of vendors being engaged in prostitution, interviews with prostitutes in Negril conducted for the ILO sponsored study previously mentioned, found that some were between 12 and 18 years (Dunn 2000). All were attracted to Negril because of the possibility of earning "good money". Some had migrated to the area and lived in the low-income areas of the community while others were migrant workers – coming in to do business then moving on. Some of the children worked as go-go dancers, prostitutes and masseuses to supplement their families' incomes. As previously noted, it is likely that some of them are among the group of male and female prostitutes that remain in active contact with or harass visitors.

Length of time in tourism

The majority of the vendors interviewed (66 percent) had been working in the tourism sector for over 5 years, and of these, 37.5 percent had worked in the industry for more than 10 years (see Table 8.2). The results suggested

Table 8.2: Length of Time in Tourism

Period Worked	%
Less than one year	7.1
1–2 years	10.7
3–5 years	16.1
6–10 years	28.6
Over 10 years	37.5
Total	100

Source: Dunn and Dunn (Survey data)

that fewer people had entered the vending trade in the last five years, which was consistent with the views of students who, as previously noted, regarded it as a last resort for employment. Although these results indicate that the market was saturated, this did not emerge as a deterrent to would-be entrants.

Job satisfaction

Most of the established vendors interviewed (80 percent) indicated that they would remain in the business for the next five years, and almost all (95 percent) said that they liked their job. The majority (71 percent) also stated that they were proud to work in tourism. However, a third of them (33 percent) admitted that there were some aspects that they disliked. Among these were: the perception that tourists were 'mean', and the attitude of some tourists who "acted like they think they are better than us". These negative views underscore the unfulfilled roles and expectations ascribed by vendors to tourists which is that they should purchase the goods and services at the prices established by the vendors. Tourists are perceived as 'mean' if they are not willing to spend money.

It also highlights the economic disparity and income levels between vendors and visitors. The second observation that tourists "acted like they are better than us" also underlies social distance between the two groups. No doubt the two perceptions are related as the economic distance may influence the social distance. There is also an unequal power relationship between the two that is resented. Vendors depend on the patronage and support of visitors for their livelihood. When they are 'mean' it has a negative impact on their standard of living, hence the resentment. This 'dependence' especially in an environment where there are sometimes more vendors than purchasers breeds resentment. While not explicit, race is no doubt also a factor as most visitors are white and vendors are black. They may therefore resent the dependence on whites to enable them to survive.

The behaviour of tourists varies widely and many of them are products of societies that practise racial discrimination against people of colour. The reaction of vendors may therefore reflect behaviours and attitudes communicated to them by some visitors in normal social interaction as they attempt to do business. There is also the possibility that they are abrasive and defensive in rejecting the approaches of persistent vendors. Understanding harassment obviously needs more in-depth research to unravel and analyse these attitudes and behaviours of both visitors and locals. This interaction may more accurately reflect the earlier definition of harassment, which perceives the visitor as an enemy or opponent. The comments of the vendors again underscore the need to improve infrastructure and living standards for locals. Daily comparison of their own modest social status with the very high status of the visitor staying in a luxury hotel and having money to spend may generate feelings of low self-esteem or resentment. The visitor comes to the vendor's stall to look and hopefully to buy something, suggesting they have money to spend. For a vendor, just trying to 'make ends meet' can be an activity which may be tinged with some sense of servitude. In the 1994 study, craft vending was the main source of income for nearly all of those interviewed (91 percent) and they sold all year round. Despite this, 71 percent of those interviewed had other skills suggesting that they could do other jobs if the opportunities presented themselves and they were able to earn comparable levels of income.

Expanding a micro-enterprise credit and training programme in Negril, could reduce the number of vendors selling similar products and create new income generating opportunities.

Income and expenditure

Few people responded to the questions relating to income and expenditure. This was not surprising as such information is considered very private. However, analysis of data for those who responded suggests the need to strengthen training in small business management, especially bookkeeping. Most vendors indicated that their expenditure exceeded their income, but that they were able to survive and continue trading. The emerging scenario was that they were either subsidising the business, they were unable to determine whether their business was making money, they were withholding details out of concern for taxation and privacy or they were not sufficiently motivated to explore other opportunities to earn a living. The reality that the majority of vendors are women must again be underscored. The women's business skills and creativity have obviously enabled them to survive. Small business training opportunities for them should be expanded. The Centre for Gender and Development Studies at the UWI has developed a training course and manual designed specifically for women micro-entrepreneurs. Industry officials may wish to explore collaboration with the Centre in the use of these resources in the industry.

Residence

The 1994 study confirmed that the majority of established vendors (52 percent) lived outside Negril and that nearly a half (48 percent) resided in and around Negril. The most common areas were Red Ground, Nonpareil Road and Capture Land, which are low-income communities. Residential patterns were unchanged in 2001, and the data were consistent with those from the Carrying Capacity Study (Hayle and Associates 2000; Boxill 2000).

Transportation

In both the 1994 and 2001 studies, close to one-half of the vendors who lived outside Negril commuted daily. This was confirmed from observations of crowded bus stops in the evenings with hundreds of people waiting for transportation in the direction of Savannah-la-Mar and Hanover. In 1994 interviews also revealed that transportation services were very poor and were a major problem for commuters as many experienced several hours delay in commuting to and from work daily. While the minibus was the main mode of transportation for 40 percent of vendors, several also had to take taxis to get home, and as such paid a high cost for transportation.

The transportation problem was further exacerbated when the gender composition of the vendors group was considered. Most were women with dependent children, which meant that the poor transportation system had a negative impact on their domestic and childcare responsibilities. Poor transportation made their workday longer, as they had to leave home early and return late from work. The quality of care provided for young children and the support given to older children also need to be considered. Some of the children of these vendors may therefore have been 'at risk' of neglect, abuse and deprivation. These factors, in turn, would have an overall negative impact on child development as well as on national development in the long term. The need for childcare offered business opportunities for women as alternatives to vending. Support to providing this service should be considered by industry policy makers and planners as well as hoteliers. Childcare should be considered an integral part of the social infrastructure required to make tourism more sustainable in Negril and in other resort communities.

Transportation problems also increased the security risks for women vendors who lived outside of Negril and had to travel for part of the journey alone or very late at night. Some reported spending hours commuting in the mornings and a similar length of time in the evenings. Persons coming from Negril's West End faced the additional challenge of getting transportation to the Negril roundabout then finding transportation in the direction of either Savannah-la-Mar or Hanover. High transportation costs may also have been a factor indirectly contributing to harassment as it increased the need for earning an income adequate to cover high living expenses, including transportation costs.

In 2001, access to transportation had improved with the introduction and expansion of legal 'route' taxis and illegal 'robots' as a business. These taxis enabled several passengers to pile into a car at a low cost and get to most destinations more quickly. However, transportation was still a problem, as stiff competition between drivers encouraged speeding as each tried to out-perform the other in securing passengers, with the additional risk of accidents.

Range and quality of goods sold

Visitors often purchase local craft items when they visit a country. Souvenirs provide a link with the country, its people and local culture. In Negril visitors seeking to purchase craft were often harassed. In an attempt to understand the problem, we examined both the range and quality of the goods being sold by established vendors and asked them to rate the quality of their goods. The comparison was interesting and provided insight into possible solutions.

Observations revealed that the range of items being sold in established locations fell into two broad categories: craft combined with clothing and food combined with drink. Some vendors specialised in one group or the other, while others sold a combination of craft items. However in general, craft and food items were not mixed. A few craft vendors specialised in wooden carvings while others sold accessories, t-shirts and other items of clothing. About 10 percent specialised in shell or leather craft and jewellery.

An analysis of the vendors was done and observations of products being sold were made to determine if men and women sold similar or different kinds of items. The results showed that while both men and women sold a combination of craft and souvenir items, women were more likely to sell wooden carvings and craft than men, accounting for 66 percent and 34 percent respectively. Women accounted for 80 percent and men 20 percent of those who sold clothing. The food and drink market was however dominated by men with 67 percent of males and 33 percent of females selling these items.

Perceptions of quality

In trying to understand harassment as it related to vending, the 1994 study tried to determine whether vendors' perceptions of the quality of their craft items were associated with exerting pressure on visitors to purchase items. Nearly all vendors rated the quality of their items as 'good' or 'excellent' but observations revealed that the quality of craft products varied – suggesting the need for training in quality control (Table 8.3).

Table 8.3: Vendors' Craft Rating

Rating	%
Excellent	44
Good	50
Average	6
Total	100

Source: Dunn and Dunn (Survey data)

Another factor considered was the cost of craft and related items, as "high prices" was one of the factors identified by tourists as a deterrent. The research probes tried to determine if price in relation to the quality of goods on sale was high and if vendors felt under pressure to harass visitors to purchase their goods as volume sales were not at the levels desired.

Observations of craft items revealed a lack of diversity and poor quality of goods, which reflected negatively on Jamaica's tourism product. This was especially unfortunate against the background of the high cost being demanded for poor quality goods. These factors, we hypothesized, increased competition in the market which in turn created more pressure on both vendors and visitors. The vendors exert pressure on visitors to buy and the visitors while searching for acceptable souvenirs, resist buying goods that to them are costly and of poor quality. Lack of training or inadequate experience in pricing, costing and marketing of goods added fuel to fire that may have contributed to harassment.

This gap between the perceptions of vendors and visitors as it related to the quality and cost of goods could be addressed by ensuring that vendors are trained to diversify the range and improve the quality and cost of their goods. Some of this activity was already underway through the programmes of the Tourism Product Development Company Ltd (TPDCo). Exposing vendors to craft items from other countries would enable them to understand the comparisons that visitors make when they are asked to purchase local craft items. This could be achieved by their participation in or attending international trade fairs. Improving the quality and cost of items would engender a more equitable business exchange between vendor and visitor that would offer better value for money. Diversifying craft will also promote choice and reduce competition between vendors.

In seeking solutions, the study also tried to identify some of the cost factors associated with the production of the craft and other items on sale. The findings revealed that 66 percent of vendors bought raw materials and produced the items they sold, whereas 30 percent were traders who bought and sold ready-made goods. Craft producers were more likely to rate the quality of their goods highly. Although only a few rated their products as "excellent" it is possible that they too may exert pressure on visitors to purchase their goods, to cover their high production costs.

Vendors who produced their own craft also reported that they had to go far afield to get raw materials. While a few of these items could be purchased in Negril, they had to travel for approximately half and hour to Savannah-la-Mar which was the main shopping town. Others reported that they had to go as far as Clarendon, Kingston and Montego Bay to get wood from saw mills and to purchase cloth or cotton for clothing and accessories. Transportation costs had to be added to the cost of raw materials which were no doubt reflected in the final prices. There was also the possibility that having had to expend considerable money and effort to produce their goods, the value placed on them was high. At the same time, the price of the products may not be competitive and visitors complained about the high cost of goods.

In addition to training, the establishment of a buying cooperative among certain producer groups could help to reduce production costs and ensure the availability of raw materials within the community. Many vendors in the plazas reported that they had received training from the tourism authorities. This was however aimed at improving their attitudes to and interaction with tourists as well as facilitating production. The study therefore sought to determine whether exposure to training had helped them generally and had also helped to reduce harassment. The results showed that training had been widespread and did have a positive impact. Within the Cotton Tree and Negril Vendors' Plaza, all the men and women interviewed indicated that they had received training and that this had been useful. As expected, a larger number of women vendors reported that they had received training and most recalled the course they had attended.

The six most frequently cited areas of training were how to relate to tourists, small business management, selling techniques, bookkeeping, marketing and how to keep the environment clean. Some vendors also recalled receiving training from the management of the Vendors' Plaza in how to display goods, while others reported success in marketing goods to tourists as a result of training provided by the Tourism Action Plan (TAP).

In addition to the training in quality control, product diversity and costing, proposed training in batik craft emerged as a special area of interest expressed by some women. They however raised the problems of access to credit, training and production sites as being among the possible obstacles. Another marketing idea that emerged was linking production sites to marketing outlets, with the possibility of merging these and offering them as centres of interest to tourists. In so doing, this could provide additional visitor attractions within the craft sector. As one vendor observed, the craft markets should be both outlets for products and locations to showcase local productivity and ways of life.

Focus group discussions were held with established vendors located in the Vendors' Plaza. Building this facility had enabled 55 vendors to be relocated from the streets, most of whom were members of the Itinerant Vendors Association. During focus group discussions with the tenants over the periods October 1994 and April 2001, it emerged that while tourist harassment had been considerably reduced, it still occurred. This group of vendors however understood that harassment was bad for business. They voiced concerns about the need to find space for other vendors who could not be accommodated in the Plaza.

Other training needs were identified from these discussions: training in leadership, group dynamics, strategic planning, collective marketing and negotiation skills. The latter emerged from vendors' concerns about the poor marketing of the Plaza to the hotels and their perceptions that hoteliers were promoting the Plaza in a lukewarm manner to their guests. This perception may also have contributed to visitor harassment, as the most had to be made from the few tourists who ventured into the arcades. However, no causal link between limited visitor numbers and harassment was established.

There was also general recognition that reducing visitor harassment among the population of vendors in Negril was also contingent on finding suitable accommodation for all vendors and upgrading the facilities at the Negril Craft Village. It was physically unattractive and became severely flooded when it rained.

Vendors' perceptions

Vendor's responses to the questionnaire showed that they perceived visitor harassment, crime and violence, illegal drugs, high prices and garbage as the five most common factors that discouraged visitors from returning to Negril (Table 8.4).

Responses to the follow-up study in 2001 indicated that vendors still perceived visitor harassment as the most important factor discouraging visitors from returning to Negril. In rank order, high prices for goods, crime and violence, garbage/litter and poor quality water followed in terms of importance. Vendors' understanding of harassment was not entirely consistent with the views of touts. Neither was their view of what constitutes harassment consistent with those of visitors or hoteliers. Touts differed from vendors as

Table 8.4 Deterrents to Visitors: Vendors' Perceptions

Ranking of Deterrents	% (1994)
Visitor Harassment	25.3
Crime and Violence	19.1
Illegal Drugs	17
High Prices	10.3
Garbage/Litter	6.2
Poor Quality Water	5.7
Poor Drainage	5.2
Other	11.2
Total	100

Source: Dunn and Dunn (Survey data)

they felt it was their right to earn a living from the tourists and for some, it was by whatever means possible. Vendors who had been exposed to training knew they should not hassle tourists to buy their goods. Boxill (2000) notes that "when asked what they thought was meant by harassment, most craft vendors said physical things like pulling and pushing the tourists. None thought it also meant to constantly badger tourists to come to their stalls. They did not believe in allowing the tourist to just stroll by on their own and choose the stall they felt like buying from for themselves" (p. 31).

Variations in the views of touts and vendors may be accounted for by several factors. Gender is definitely one as most of the touts are male while most of the vendors are female. Males also tend to be more aggressive than females in asserting themselves and voicing their demands. Age is another factor that explains this difference. The touts tend to be young men under 20 years of age, while the vendors are older – between their mid-twenties and late forties. Educational difference may also be a factor, although variations in educational backgrounds were not very wide. The vendors also operated in a more formal and structured environment that was more amenable to training, education and regulation. It was therefore easier to control their behaviour with peer pressure sometimes being an effective means of sanction. Touts on the other hand had free rein to do as they pleased and to approach whoever they wished. These are some of the factors that may account for the differing perceptions of harassment between vendors and touts.

Reasons tourists visit Jamaica: Vendors' perceptions

Vendors felt that the most important reasons why tourists come to Negril were the beaches, friendly Jamaicans, the sunsets, the scenery and the laid-back atmosphere, in rank order (Table 8.5). Few felt that Jamaican craft and souvenirs influenced their choice. This was possibly true as vendors felt that they got the last round of spending after accommodation and food, transportation, attractions and entertainment. Nevertheless, tourists' purchase of craft was important to the Negril population as it provided a source of income for hundreds of people.

In conclusion, this profile of established vendors helped to identify several factors that may contribute to visitor harassment. Economic pressures, limited alternatives for employment, a high level of competition associated with lack of variety in the range of goods sold and high production costs all emerged as important factors that may contribute to harassment.

An analysis of the gender composition of both groups of vendors revealed some important differences. The group of established vendors consisted mainly of single women between 25 and 49 years old with dependent children.

Table 8.5   Reasons Tourists Visit Jamaica: Vendors' Perceptions

Reasons	%
Beaches	22.7
Friendly Jamaicans	15.2
Sunset	12.3
Scenery	11.8
Laid Back Atmosphere	11.4
Water Sports	9.5
Craft/Souvenirs	8.5
Other	8.5
Total	100

Source: Dunn and Dunn (Survey data)

Employment opportunities were limited because of their low-levels of education. The majority had either an all-age/secondary school, or primary school education. Most had been in the business for over 10 years selling craft items which they produced for tourists, but high transportation costs and limited training and skill made it difficult for them to calculate production costs or profitability. Most of them sold a narrow range of craft items although some bought and sold clothing and accessories to supplement their stock. In general, they were satisfied with their work as vendors, but lamented the long hours spent commuting to and from home and work each day, while trying to balance their family responsibilities. These vendors had a high level of awareness that harassment was bad for business and observations of these established locations revealed little evidence of harassment.

Profile of itinerant vendors

The profile of itinerant vendors emerged from interviews and observations. Itinerant vendors were defined as roving traders, with no fixed places of business, and who sell a variety of products to both tourists and local residents. Because these vendors were so widely dispersed and highly mobile, it was not easy to get a collective or uniform assessment of them. However, because of their frequent and direct interaction with visitors they were considered an important target group in any strategy aimed at reducing visitor harassment and restricting illegal trading activities in the community.

During the survey 25 itinerant vendors were interviewed. Pre-testing indicated a high level of unwillingness to respond to questionnaires or any other formal method of data gathering. Not surprisingly they were very suspicious of any efforts to collect information and saw this as potentially increasing pressure on them from the police and industry officials. Within the limited time available for these studies, a snapshot of cases and an overview of their working methods were developed.

This profile showed that the majority of itinerant vendors in Negril were males, ranging in age from as young as 12 years to over 50 years. Most were in the age range of 21–35 years. Among this group of vendors, the older women tended to work as traders in fruit and vegetables while younger women were observed plying the streets particularly at nights and appeared to be soliciting clients as prostitutes. Among this group of men and women, nearly 60 percent were from outside of Negril – mainly from the neighbouring towns of Savannah-la-Mar, Lucea, Esher, Little London, Grange Hill, Green Island and Bluefields. Many others commuted long distances from Black River, Mandeville, Montego Bay and Kingston.

Itinerant vendors from Kingston and the more distant towns tried to sell 'dry goods' to locals. They reported selling craft items to visitors, store owners and stall operators. The items included blank audio cassettes, music tapes, shoes, cosmetics, watches, children's clothing and t-shirts. Vendors from the adjoining rural or urban communities were selling unfinished carvings, shells, craft items, fruit and vegetables. The latter included bananas, oranges, mangoes, sugar cane, herbs and spices, aloe vera and seasonings.

Local youth, as well as some of the traders from outside tried to sell necklaces, rings, earrings, brooches and pins, belts and other small, light craft items made from wood, wire, beads and strings. These items of merchandise were easily concealed in small travel bags, pouches or pockets to avoid detection or prosecution. Small, lightweight items proved to be also convenient for youths who sold their merchandise on the beaches.

Besides trading these items, many of the itinerant vendors used small quantities of the craft products as a basis for approaching visitors to offer other items and services for sale, such as drugs, sex and tour guide services. Not only were they versatile in the range of services offered but also creative in the locations from which items or services were offered. Their mobility allowed them to quickly move to locations where tourists congregate. The absence of any significant overhead expenses meant that they were able to offer products at cheaper rates than vendors in the plazas with stalls or store operators were able to. Their presence in Negril created tensions among operators in fixed locations, as itinerant vendors sometimes followed tourists into the markets and arcades, offering them goods already on sale in these locations.

Analysis of the profiles and perceptions of these two groups of vendors shows that the established regulated vendors are more likely to be women, who are trained and aware that harassment is bad for business. The itinerant vendors tend to be male who by definition are mobile and sell a range of items to locals as well as tourists. Unlike their colleagues who have a fixed place of operation and are required to adhere to the rules of the plazas, the itinerant vendors were unregulated and difficult to control. In the 2001 study, these vendors were under pressure from increased police presence in Negril. An expansion in the number of police officers at the station, partly related to security upgrades for Spring Break, has resulted in a reduction in the number of itinerant vendors. However, this situation is regarded as a form of temporary suppression and did not appear to reflect any real reduction in their activity. Different strategies would therefore be required, including training and public education programmes for these traders, aimed at reducing visitor harassment.

9

Workers in Negril

Profiles and Perceptions

Profile of workers

Workers in the tourism industry are often the first and most accessible persons with whom visitors interact. Their performance and perceptions are therefore vital in providing an understanding of visitor harassment. This chapter examines the findings from a sample of 106 workers interviewed in our questionnaire survey in selected tourism related establishments in Negril. These included hotels, guesthouses, restaurants, transportation related operations and recreational facilities. Our findings provide an overview of their characteristics, attitudes and their perceptions of visitors. As with the other profiles, this information can guide the development of training and public education strategies to address the problem of visitor harassment.

Demographic profile

Sex

The 1994 study revealed that there were more males than females working in the industry. Sixty-seven percent of the workers interviewed were males and

33 percent were females. In 2001 the gender gap had narrowed, with 55 percent males and 45 percent females in the sample. These trends were consistent with the movement towards greater participation of women in the labour force and more women moving into sectors previously dominated by men.

Age

The data from the 1994 study show that the majority of workers were young people below the age of 35 years (Table 9.1). The dramatic reduction in numbers after age 35 years suggests that most workers leave the industry before age 40. Data from the 2001 study suggested that while the majority of workers were still in the age range 25–34 years (55 percent), there were fewer young people in the 18–24 years age range and more in the 35–49 age range. While the data reflected in the above Table may not be completely accurate, given sample disparities, they do indicate a trend of fewer young people coming into the sector and of a stable core of workers who have remained.

Table 9.1: Age of Workers

Age	(%) 1994	(%) 2001
18–24	41.0	27
25–34	46.7	55
35–49	9.5	18
50–64	2.8	0
Total	100	100

Source: Dunn and Dunn (Survey data)

Education

Table 9.2 shows that in 1994 the majority of workers were either graduates of a secondary/all-age school, a high school or a technical/vocational school in rank order. This presents an interesting comparison with vendors who tend to have a lower level of education. In 2001, 46 percent of workers interviewed had a high school education compared to only 27 percent in the earlier study.

Table 9.2: Educational Level of Workers

Educational Level	(%) 1994	(%) 2001
Primary	8.5	0
Technical/Vocational	18.9	18
Secondary/All-Age	31.1	36
High School	27.3	46
Other	14.2	0
Total	100	100

Source: Dunn and Dunn (Survey data)

This provided strong evidence that the industry was attracting persons with a higher level of education.

Marital status

In 1994, more than half of the workers were single (66 percent), almost 19 percent were in a visiting relationship, 12 percent were married and almost 3 percent were either divorced or separated (Table 9.3). These findings will be compared with the number of persons dependent on them.

In 2001, 72 percent of those interviewed were single (showing a significant increase), 18 percent were in a visiting relationship and 9 percent were married.

Table 9.3: Marital Status of Workers

Marital Status	(%) 1994	(%) 2001
Single	66	72
Married	12.3	9
Divorced/Separated	2.8	1
Visiting Relationship	18.9	18
Total	100	100

Source: Dunn and Dunn (Survey data)

Dependents

The sample was fairly evenly split between workers who did and did not have dependent relatives. The majority of the 51 percent who did, supported either one or two persons.

Approximately 60 percent of the workers had dependent children (Table 9.4). The data suggest that most workers had heavy family commitments and that most were supporting at least two adults and two children. The pattern was also reported in the 2001 study with 36 percent of workers reporting that they had between two and three dependent adults (Table 9.5). This suggests that a larger number of persons are dependent on jobs provided by the industry for their livelihood.

Table 9.4 Number of Dependent Children

Number of Children	%
None	40
One	26
Two	18
Three or Four	10
Five	2
Six	4
Total	100

Source: Dunn and Dunn (Survey data)

Table 9.5 Number of Dependent Adults

Number of Adults	%
None	49
One	22
Two	22
Three	5
Four or more	2
Total	100

Source: Dunn and Dunn (Survey data)

Length of time in tourism

The findings of the earlier study indicated that while male workers have dominated the industry and have been employed for a longer period, more females were entering the sector and were doing so at twice the rate of males. This trend had continued. In the more recent study, half of those persons interviewed were female and half were male; 50 percent of those in the industry for less than a year were females.

Income of workers

In the earlier study there was evidence of disparity in income earned by men and women. Most male workers earned between $1,000 and $10,000 weekly while women earned between $1,000 and $5,000 weekly (Table 9.6). Forty percent of these women earned between $1,000 and $3,000. (In 1994 the exchange rate was J$35.5:US$1.00.) Higher income earners were thrice as likely to be men than women. The pattern of women receiving lower wages was consistent with the situation in several industries and requires further research.

Among the smaller sample of persons interviewed in the 2001 study, the average basic weekly wage was calculated. The results showed that males earned an average of J$3,066 (US$67) per week and women earned J$2,800 (US$62) – a difference of $268 (US$5). (In 2001 the exchange rate was approximately J$45.5:US$1.00.) This suggests that female workers are still earning less than male workers, but the wage gap identified in 1994 is closing. Male and female workers will hopefully receive equal pay for work of equal

Table 9.6: Income of Workers

Basic Pay	Male %	Female %
$1,000–$3,000 (US$28–85)	30	40
$3,100–$5,000 (US$87–141)	21	26
$5,100–$10,000 (US$144–282)	22	3
Over $10,000 (US$282)	9	3
Don't Know	18	28
Total	100	100

Source: Dunn and Dunn (Survey data, 1994)

value in the not too distant future, consistent with Jamaican laws. (In 1995 the exchange rate was J$35.5: US$1.00.)

Residence and access to transportation

In the 1994 study, most workers (like the established vendors) lived outside Negril and reported difficulties in accessing reliable transportation. The main communities in which they lived were Hartford, Shrewsbury, Lances Bay, Red Ground District in Negril and Little London in Westmoreland. In 2001, most workers reported that access to transportation was either easy or very easy. This would no doubt reflect the larger number of route taxis in operation as previously discussed in presenting the profile of vendors. Poor infrastructure for local residents was one of the factors highlighted as contributing to visitor harassment in the 1994 study.

Between the 1994 and 2001 studies, a number of riots took place in Negril. The issues which triggered some of these had been identified in the earlier study. Among these were the rental rates charged for use of craft vending facilities, and prolonged infrastructure projects such as the installation of a sewage system which severely disrupted normal vehicular and pedestrian traffic and which was a major eyesore for several years. The unequal distribution of income generated by the industry continued to be a source of tension between the 'big man' and the 'small man'– characterized by large hoteliers as opposed to small hoteliers and the majority of poor local residents. Employment opportunities had expanded with the construction of new properties, but most of this had been of all-inclusive hotels, which limit the benefits derived by local residents.

Public education programmes conducted by the industry have expanded since the 1994 study and Negril has benefited from tourism education programmes in schools with the integration of tourism in the school curriculum. Negril has benefited from several other industry programmes. These include: the Resort Security Programme which was introduced to combat crime and visitor harassment, the Programme for the Resettlement and Integrated Development Enterprises (PRIDE) created to deal with squatter communities, and the Sustaining the Environment and Tourism (SET) Project, which was introduced to address environmental degradation. In 1996–97, TPDCo received a 37 percent budget increase to J$300m to improve the physical facilities in resort areas.

The Northern Coastal Highway Improvement Project linking Negril to Montego Bay has also been a major infrastructure project. So too is the Negril Water Supply project. Both were funded under the Northern Jamaica Development Project (NJDP), an initiative aimed at addressing inadequate road and sewage infrastructure in the main economic centres of northern Jamaica. In 1997, the industry embarked on a programme to develop a Ten-Year Tourism Master Plan that covered three phases: Industry Diagnosis, the Formulation of Strategic Options and Tourism Action Planning (Planning Institute of Jamaica 1996, 1997, 1998).

Frequently workers have highlighted the need for low-income housing, jobs in other industries, an improved water supply system and garbage collection as the most important services that were in need of improvement for residents and workers in Negril. The findings of the 2001 study showed that despite the many efforts by government and private sector, many of these concerns raised by workers in the earlier study had not been adequately addressed.

Perceptions of enabling and inhibiting factors for visitors

The initial study tried to determine the perceptions and attitudes of workers to visitors and tourists in order to determine if this had an impact on visitor harassment. The findings from the questionnaires are presented below.

In the 1994 study workers perceived the beaches as the most important attraction for tourists, with friendly Jamaicans, the scenery, the sunset and

Table 9.7 Reasons Tourists Visit: Workers' Perceptions

Ranking of Reasons	Percentage
Beaches	26
Friendly Jamaicans	15
Scenery	14
Sunset	14
Laid-back Atmosphere	14
Culture	10
Water Sports	5
Other	2
Total	100

Source: Dunn and Dunn (Survey data)

Negril's laid-back atmosphere having almost equal weight and importance (Table 9.7). In the 2001 study the pattern was slightly altered with friendly Jamaicans, beaches, laid-back atmosphere, breathtaking sunset, beautiful scenery and culture emerging as the five most important reasons in rank order. By highlighting the Jamaican people, this response suggests a greater awareness of the importance of people to tourism.

Table 9.8   Workers' Attitudes to Tourism and Tourists

Ranking of Workers' Attitudes	%
Proud to Work in Tourism	50.3
Tourism Created Many Jobs	42.2
Can't Do Better	4.1
Waiting to Migrate/Other	2
Tourism Brought Problems	1.4
Total	100

Source: Dunn and Dunn (Survey data)

Workers' attitudes to visitors were explored and the results are presented in Table 9.8.

Data from the 1994 study showed that workers' attitudes to tourism and tourists were overwhelmingly positive. Half of them (50.3 percent) said they were proud to work in tourism and 42 percent felt that it had created a lot of jobs. In the follow-up study in 2001, these two attitudes remained consistently positive. At the same time there is a high turnover among employees who have recently started working in the industry. This suggests that management-worker relations may need to be reviewed. The findings indicate the need for further research.

Efforts were also made to determine workers' perceptions of harassment and to assess whether these perceptions were influenced by the length of time they had worked in the industry (Table 9.9).

The results showed that while most workers agreed that tourist harassment was a major problem, those who had been in the industry for a longer period held stronger views on the extent of the problem. Results of the 2001 study confirmed that the majority of workers still perceived visitor harassment as a

Table 9.9 Workers' Perceptions of Harassment by Length of Service

Perceptions of Harassment	<1 year	1–2 years	3–4 years	Over 5 years
Strongly Agree	40	33	69	74
Agree	60	56.	14	18
Disagree	0	11	17	5
Strongly Disagree	0	0	0	3
Total	100	100	100	100

Source: Dunn and Dunn (Survey data)

major problem; and 92 percent either agreed or strongly agreed that visitor harassment was a problem in Negril.

Training

Table 9.10 shows that workers had been exposed to a variety of training courses provided by TAP and TPDCo. The majority had received training in tourism awareness while others had been exposed to environmental education and foreign language courses. The considerable investment in training on tourism awareness appeared to have been an effective deterrent to visitor harassment by workers.

The findings also suggested a strong correlation between exposure to general training courses and length of service. Forty percent of those who had worked in the industry for over five years had been exposed to some form of

Table 9.10 Workers' Training and Length of Time Employed

Training	<1 year	1–2 years	3–4 years	Over 5 years
Tourism Awareness	67	79	73	69
Foreign Language	17	21	8	37
Clean Environment	0	36	19	43
Other	17	7	35	40

Source: Dunn and Dunn (Survey data)

training. Interviews with workers also helped to identify a number of areas in which training needed to be expanded to support their career aspirations.

Workers' career aspirations – Implications for training

Workers were asked what other kinds of work they would like to do if they had a choice. Their responses gave an indication of their career aspirations. Most selected work areas with a higher social, skill-level and income status. Their responses have been summarised as a guide for personnel departments and planners in the industry. Housekeepers said they would like to do nursing, dressmaking, data-entry, typing and waiter services, which suggested a higher level of skill. Waiters and waitresses expressed interest in studying food and nutrition, language training, nursing, computing, front desk and management skills, as well as electrical engineering.

Bartenders indicated an interest in computer skills, hotel management, entrepreneurship and business management, cashiering, language training, training to become a waiter or chef, electrical installation, electrical engineering, building, or construction skills.

Given a choice, security guards would seek to get training in electrical engineering, police work, foreign languages, agriculture, driving, or enhanced security skills.

Billing clerks wanted to study accounting, to become receptionists, to acquire computer or typing skills, or to become tour guides. Cashiers expressed interest in becoming receptionists. A bike rental worker wanted to study auto body repairs.

Several of these work categories provided scope for training and job re-design, to partially fulfil the aspirations of jobholders. For example, housekeepers could be given short-term first aid courses, and share some of the responsibility for first aid with nursing and medical staff. A housekeeper interested in dressmaking could have her job re-designed to include responsibility for minor repairs to sheets, pillowcases and curtains. Similarly, training in computer skills would ensure that over time, a housekeeper could become computer-literate and competent to assist with office duties or could rotate when necessary. Job rotation and multi-skilling could become a key strategy for training in small as well as large establishments. The general manager of one of the larger hotels reported that this principle was used at their hotel to create awareness of how various work activities are interlinked.

Overall, the findings indicate that employment in the tourism industry is a stepping stone to other careers. Tourism officials could use this information to formulate policies and programmes designed to strengthen collaboration with training institutions and to reduce the attrition rate of skilled workers in the industry.

Perception of deterrents

Consistent with the approach used for consulting with vendors, workers in the industry were asked to share their views on the main factors that discourage visitors from returning to Negril (Table 9.11). Their responses are summarised below.

Like the established vendors, those workers consulted in the 1994 study felt that harassment was the main deterrent to visitors returning for a holiday. In rank order, the other main reasons were: illegal drugs, crime and violence, and high prices. The follow-up study done in 2001 found that workers still perceived visitor harassment as the number one deterrent, followed by high prices, raw sewage on beaches, crime and violence, and illegal drugs.

These findings suggested that although workers still perceive harassment as the major problem, their interface with visitors suggested to them that their clients were also put off by high prices and raw sewage. The problem of sewage was associated with delays in completing the Negril sewage infrastructure project.

Table 9.11 Deterrents to Visitors: Workers' Perceptions

Ranking of Deterrents	%
Visitor Harassment	24.3
Illegal Drugs	18.8
Crime and Violence	16.8
High Prices	11.8
Garbage and Litter	7.7
Poor Water Quality	5
Sewage on Beach	4.8
Other	10.8
Total	100

Source: Dunn and Dunn (Survey data)

In concluding this section, the emerging profile of workers in the tourism sector was a group that was overwhelmingly male. However, over the years more gender balance emerged in the workforce – although the more recent survey in 2001 suggested that there was still a gender imbalance in favour of males. The second characteristic emerging was that the majority of workers were young adults, between 25 and 35 years old. The age profile of the industry suggested that people enter, stay for awhile then leave. These characteristics have implications for developing a service culture in the industry. Workers are integral to this process and trainers will therefore need to take account of the different factors that motivate male workers as opposed to female workers.

A comparison of data collected for 1994 and 2001 suggested that the industry had recently been attracting and recruiting more educated persons. While the majority of workers interviewed in 1994 had a secondary or all-age school education, most of those in 2001 had a high school education, especially those who had been employed for less than a year. This was understandable as most of the new recruits were women, and was therefore consistent with the national trend of women being more likely than men to take advantage of educational opportunities. The women were usually single with dependents. Most of them had an average of two to three adults and between one and six children who depended on them for support. This implied that the wages of many workers had to feed a family of five.

During the period between the two surveys, residence outside Negril had become less of a problem as transportation services had improved. However, workers cited the need for low-income housing and good infrastructure as major challenges. This is consistent with observations by Boxill (2000) that reflected the views of squatters in Negril.

Training and education emerged as important factors that help to reduce visitor harassment. Most workers reported that they had received considerable training in tourism awareness, suggesting that the industry had invested heavily in training. This no doubt contributed to a lower incidence of harassment among workers than expected if many were residents of the communities inside and outside Negril.

Higher levels of education made workers more capable of exploring and conceptualising alternative work choices than was the situation with vendors. No doubt, higher education had helped them to develop more logical and analytical skills than their compatriots with lower levels of education. This would have made them better able to understand the negative impact that harassment would have on visitors and on their own job stability. Lower levels of harassment among workers could also have been related to that fact that the majority of those interviewed expressed satisfaction with their job and acknowledged the importance of tourism for employment. Higher education, job satisfaction and positive attitudes therefore appeared to reduce visitor harassment.

The implications for the industry are that the educational (and skill) level of workers needs to be constantly upgraded and the policy of recruiting workers with higher levels of education should be maintained. The findings also suggest that management in the industry will also have to change to be able to deal with a workforce that is more highly educated and therefore mobile. With a higher level of education, workers will move on to other jobs outside the tourism sector if working conditions are unsatisfactory and if there is limited scope for mobility. Training workers who will then use the industry as a stepping stone to other jobs outside the sector will not be cost-effective. Industry planners therefore need to ensure that the sector retains the brightest and best recruits by ensuring that management practices and the industrial relations climate are conducive to employment sustainability. It is even more important as visitors reported that they returned to specific properties because they know the staff and the staff knows them, as well as their likes and dislikes. Workers and worker satisfaction are therefore central to building a service culture in the tourism sector.

As currently structured, the industry can only accommodate a small number of high achievers rising to management and supervisory levels. From our assessment, the others will have to seek employment in other sectors at mid-career, in order to generate income levels required by their growing family size. There is some movement of staff from full-time employment in the sector to own-account businesses, as some people go into small guest house operations or into supply and support services. The others may be lost to the industry despite considerable knowledge accumulated. The challenge facing tourism industry planners is to monitor the process of staff movement and plan optimum methods of retaining their services, either in full-time employment within the sector or through businesses that support tourism. TPDCo as part of its policy should continue to support training to retain workers to the ultimate benefit of the industry.

CHAPTER 10

Tourists Visiting Negril

Profiles and Perceptions

Profile of tourists in Negril

The profile of tourists presented in this chapter was developed from question-naires administered to overseas visitors in 1994 and 2001. The aim was to get information on the characteristics of visitors that came to Negril, their views on the harassment problem and to identify factors contributing to harassment. This data can guide hoteliers and industry planners as they try to promote a more service oriented culture.

Sex

Most of those interviewed in 1994 were males (76 percent); 24 percent were females. In the 2001 study, 73 percent were males and 27 percent were females, suggesting that Negril attracted more males than females.

Age

The largest group of visitors was young working adults between 25 and 34 years old (35 percent) followed by mature working adults between 35 and 49 years (30 percent). Fewer of them were young adults 18–24 years (26 percent) and less than 10 percent were over 50 years. This suggested that Negril tended to attract working adults between 25 and 49 years who needed a break from work rather than retired persons. In recent years however, Negril had also attracted a new kind of visitor in the form of young college students who visited during their Spring Break. These no doubt accounted for the age group between 18 and 24 years. Industry planners and marketers will therefore need to take account of what Negril has to offer to each of these age groups as visitors come for different packages of accommodation and attractions (Dunn and Dunn 1999). Analysis of the data from the 2001 study showed almost equal numbers of persons aged 25–34 (36.4 percent) and 50–64 years (34.6 percent) and some younger people aged 18–25 (27.2 percent).

Marital status

In the 1994 study there were more married than single persons. More than half of those interviewed (58 percent) were married or living with a partner while 42 percent were single. Data from the 2001 study however showed a reversal of this trend; 58 percent were single and 42 percent were married. The latter survey reflected the higher number of seasonal college students in the visitor population. The overall conclusion however was that Negril was attractive to both younger couples and singles seeking a laid-back holiday destination.

Education, income and occupation

Harassment was associated with persons who had an economic motive. The study therefore sought to determine the occupational background of visitors as a clue to their economic status. More than half of those interviewed in 1994 were professionals (52 percent) or had a secondary school education (57 percent); one-third (32 percent) had been to college or university; and one-quarter had technical jobs (26 percent). Against this background, it was not surprising that 40 percent of those interviewed had an annual income of between US$40,000–75,000. One-third earned between US$20,000 and US$40,000. While their actual income would not be known by the average Negril resident, the fact that they could afford a holiday implied that they had money to spend and were therefore potential targets for harassment.

In the 2001 study, half (50 percent) were professionals, 37.5 percent were students and 12.5 percent were retired. The pattern was consistent with the majority being professionals – more so if the retired persons are added to this group. In the 2001 study over half (55 percent) had been to university, 36 percent had been to college and 9 percent had a high school education. More visitors therefore had higher education (96 percent) but their income patterns had shifted: 45.4 percent earned less than US$20,000, 36.4 percent, just over a third earned between US$20,000–39,000 and only 18.2 percent earned over US$40,000. This explained the perception of workers and vendors that "high prices" were an important deterrent to visitors returning to Negril. The figures for 2001 also reflect the presence of college students on Spring Break.

Nationality/Country of origin

Nationality is an important factor in planning for and marketing tourism. Most visitors interviewed in 1994 were from Europe (64 percent), while 36 percent were from North America. These included Italians, Germans and persons from the United Kingdom.

Hayle and Associates (2000) include an analysis of market segmentation drivers and dislikes of visitors by nationality. While the findings were not sex-disaggregated, the nationality profile emerging from their 1999 study showed that persons from the United States wanted value for money and were attracted to all-inclusive hotels that were family oriented. They came for sun, sea and sand and enjoyed aquatic sports. They tended to take short holidays in winter or spring and valued familiarity with foods, accommodation and entertainment. They disliked crime and harassment.

Visitors from the United Kingdom also came seeking sun, sea and sand but also wanted adventure and variety. They preferred packaged tours and usually added 3–4 side tours. For accommodation, they wanted luxury, preferred all-inclusive hotels but also wanted value for money. They were described as 'price sensitive'. Once familiar with the market, they were likely to return. Visitor harassment and personal safety were also important issues for them.

German visitors were described as well educated, aged 20+ or 40–49 years, with high disposable incomes. They preferred packaged tours and added 3–4 side tours. They tended to visit during the winter break and stayed about three weeks. The attraction for them was relaxation, sun, sand, sea, hiking, nature and interaction with local people. Dislikes for them were prices, the lack of large European Plan properties, harassment and lack of personal safety.

Hayle (2000) noted that Italian visitors were independent travellers with high disposable income. They preferred upscale accommodation but wanted value for money. They tended to take long holidays. Attractions for them were interaction with local people, the variety of foods, entertainment, heritage and culture and good shopping. Italians disliked packaged tours, high prices, harassment, poor product experiences outside the hotels and were concerned about personal safety (Hayle and Associates 2000: 46). The main issue emerging from Hayle's analysis is that regardless of nationality, visitor harassment was disliked by tourists.

The majority of tourists interviewed in our study (67 percent), were first-time visitors. Only a small core of 15 percent constituted regular visitors and most of them (61 percent) had been referred by friends. If first-timers were exposed to harassment, there was the risk that they were unlikely to return or recommend Jamaica to their friends.

The trend in the country of origin had shifted in 2001; 54.5 percent of visitors were from North America, most of whom were from the USA and 45.5 percent were from Europe. Of these, 83 percent were first time visitors and 17 percent were frequent visitors. Fifty-eight percent said that referrals by friends and relatives who had visited Negril were the most important factor influencing their decision to come for a holiday. Travel agencies had influenced another 25 percent and the remaining 17 percent who checked "other" had done their research on the internet. None of those interviewed in the sample indicated that their choice of destination had been influenced by JTB advertisements.

Planning and marketing implications of the visitor profile

The 2001 study confirmed the pattern of a dominance of male visitors (67 percent) most of whom were professionals (42 percent) or students (25 percent). One-half (50 percent) had a university degree while one-third (33 percent) were students with a college education. More North Americans were visiting Negril as this had become a popular Spring Break destination for college students as previously noted.

Harassment, crime and violence and high prices were consistently reported as the most important deterrents, indicating a shift from the previous study in which visitor harassment was considered the most important deterrent. High prices were a major problem for older visitors. A retired Canadian visitor who was on vacation with his wife to celebrate his birthday and their anniversary underscored this point. He stated in an interview that this would be their last visit because of the very high cost of a holiday in Jamaica. As retired people, they could no longer afford a holiday here. The man noted that a night in a very good hotel in Canada cost half of what he paid in Negril. Industry planners should take note of the needs of an ageing vacationing clientele, with less disposable income for holidays.

The 1994 study confirmed that poor service was also a major deterrent to visitors. The same Canadian visitor disagreed with the wage structure of workers in their medium-sized hotel and recounted several experiences of poor service. Among the most annoying were inattention to details of meals ordered, long delays in the arrival of food, or services requested in their room. For example, a request for face towels took one week to be filled, and was done only after repeated requests. Attention to detail therefore emerged as an important area for the training of industry workers in promoting a service culture. As previously noted, many visitors like to return to the same hotel, often requested the same room, and tried to rekindle friendships with workers and management. Some asked for special services such as fruit or flowers and they liked dealing with staff members who knew their special needs. This personalised service, available especially in smaller establishments, was very highly valued and encouraged visitors to return to the Eden of Negril.

Consistent with the views expressed by visitors, the staff of many hotels and guesthouses confirmed that they depended on a core of loyal repeat visitors as their main source of income. Efforts were therefore made to provide special services to their guests and to remember their tastes and needs.

In 1994, more than half the visitors (55 percent) stayed for 7–14 days. This was understandable. Europeans tended to stay longer than North Americans because of the distance and time required for travelling to and from Jamaica. Their length of stay was consistent with the annual statistics of the JTB which showed that Americans spent an average of 8.6 nights, while visitors from the UK and other Europeans spend 20.9 nights and 14.7 nights respectively.

Harassment over a 14-day period would be enough time to convince any visitor not to return.

Most visitors stayed in properties that were not all-inclusive: 61 percent stayed in hotels, 13 percent stayed in villas, 11 percent in apartments and 2 percent in cabins. Those staying outside of the all-inclusive properties would have been more exposed to harassment. Most accommodation sites in Negril provided security around the clock to better protect their guests, but observations at a hotel at 3:00 o'clock one morning confirmed that there were no guarantees as some guests invited local people to visit their rooms.

Deterrents

The earlier study confirmed that visitor harassment was the factor most likely to deter visitors from returning to Negril (Table 10.1). Contrary to the perception that crime and violence would have been the second most important reason, visitors said that rising prices were a more important deterrent. Environmental factors such as beach pollution, poor water, sewage and drainage ranked next, followed by poor service. Tourists indicated that night-noises were not a major deterrent, a perception also shared by workers and vendors.

Table 10.1   Deterrents to Visitors: Tourists' Perceptions

Ranking of Deterrents	%
Visitor Harassment	26
Rising Prices	15
Crime and Violence	12
Beach Pollution	11
Poor Water/Sewage/Drainage	10
Garbage on Streets	8
Poor Service	6
Shacks	6
Destruction of Coral Reefs	5
Night Noises	1
Total	100

Source: Dunn and Dunn (Survey data)

In the more recent study, there had been a shift: crime and violence emerged as the primary deterrent, followed by visitor harassment and rising prices. This perception contrasts with the views of vendors and workers in the industry. This information, combined with the research by Hayle (2000) on the dislikes of specific nationalities provides yet another convincing case to eliminate harassment in Negril.

In conclusion therefore, reducing or eliminating harassment, expanding facilities and attractions for the segmented client groups, and improving the quality of service emerged as important factors for the success of the industry. Each of these involves people, and part of the strategy of industry planners should therefore engage people as partners in developing the tourism product.

Sustainability of tourism in Negril will require improved communication between ordinary community residents and industry leaders. Research, including the profile of visitors, has to be shared with local people more consistently in a form that is more easily accessible and digestible. Similarly, shifts in the Negril market need to be shared with community members and a strong partnership established with all key stakeholders. The findings of the various studies must be communicated to local people to diversify the product, improve Negril's attractiveness and eradicate the scourge of harassment. Regular channels of communication must therefore be established and maintained to keep everyone informed and involved. Local radio, television and cable channels offer some additional media outlets that can be used more creatively to spread the message. Similarly, community groups and schools are also important channels for two-way communication and dialogue.

"Tourism Time" could become a weekly programme for community television, radio or cable facilitated through a partnership between local residents, the Jamaica Tourist Board and the local business community.

11

Combatting Harassment
The Police Files

This chapter examines another dimension of the visitor harassment problem and probes deeper into the kinds of actions that were classified as "troubling or repeatedly annoying visitors" in Negril. Analysis of the Crime Diary of the Negril Police Station was used to verify the findings from the interviews and observations. This allowed us to compare, contrast and validate the information gained from the questionnaire survey, focus groups, interviews and observations.

Interviews were done with key officials in the station in 2001 and 1994 to understand the problem more explicitly. Analysis of the Crime Dairy data was done, focusing on arrests made between 1989 and 1993 and for 1999–2000. This helped to determine patterns and types of harassment, and to develop a profile and characteristics of persons who were arrested for various offences. This information provided insight into the frequency of arrests for harassment, the most common types of offences, the main locations, and the period of day or night these activities were most likely to occur. The following Tables present the findings.

Table 11.1: Pattern of Arrests for Harassment, 1991–1993; 1999–2000

Month	1991	1992	1993	1999	2000
January	54	135	111	49	91
February	48	120	123	78	70
March	91	121	99	73	88
April	50	74	51	24	40
May	66	64	40	24	57
June	47	55	100	31	65
July	72	82	103	59	91
August	85	97	86	58	147
September	79	86	103	78	122
October	57	105	129	72	62
November	77	71	113	57	109
December	108	92	112	81	52
Total	834	1,102	1,059	684	994
Monthly Average	70	92	88	57	83

Source: Compiled from Negril Police data (selected years)

The figures in Table11.1 indicate arrests made by the police in the Negril community and may not be a reflection of crimes committed overall. Negril police also acknowledged that many offenders were not arrested. Analysis revealed that there was no discernible pattern in the time of year that arrests take place, although the number of arrests peaked in 1992. The number of arrests had fluctuated in the last few years despite increased police presence in the community.

The data on categories of arrests confirmed the perception of Negril as being associated with narcotic drugs and most arrests (82 percent) were drug related, with ganja as the dominant type of drug used (Table 11.2). Only three categories of arrest were identified as being specifically related to harassment (18 percent) although it is recognized that some of the drug related arrests are also linked to the offering of drugs to visitors. 'Soliciting', 'offering goods for sale' and 'offering services' ranked third, fifth and seventh in the total ranking of offence type in Table 11.2.

Table 11.2 Types of Offences

Ranking of Types	Total
Possession of Ganja	367
Possession of Cocaine	86
Soliciting	57
Smoking Ganja	38
Exposing Goods/ Sale	37
Dealing in Ganja	32
Offering Services	27
Possession of Chillum pipe	19
Dealing in Cocaine	9
Possession of Hash Oil	2
Cultivating Ganja	2
Total	676

Source: Compiled from Negril Police data, 1994

The data show that offences occur around the clock and policing is a 24-hour job (Table 11.3).

As expected, the data confirmed that in rank order Negril Beach and the West End were the two locations where harassment was most likely to take place (Table 11.4). This understandable, as these locations are less easily

Table 11.3 Time of Arrests

Time of Arrests	Number of Arrests	%
6:00 p.m. – 11:59 p.m.	30	25
12:00 midnight – 5:59 a.m.	22	19
6:00 a.m. – 11:59 a.m.	26	22
12:00 noon – 5:59 p.m.	29	24
Not Stated/Unclear	12	10
Total	119	100

Source: Compiled from Negril Police data, 1994

Table 11.4 Place of Arrests

Time of Arrests	Number of Arrests	%
Negril Beach	44	37
West End	24	20
Norman Manley Blvd	12	10
Other Locations	39	33
Total	119	100

Source: Compiled from Negril Police data, 1994

patrolled than the Norman Manley Boulevard, which is the main road in Negril. The data from the police record also showed that although many business establishments including properties with beach-fronts have 24-hour security, 28 percent of arrests were made on private property, demonstrating that staying in a private residence may not be a deterrent to would-be harassers. An analysis was also done to develop a demographic profile of the persons prosecuted. The findings are presented below.

Profile of persons prosecuted for harassment

Sex

Among the 119 persons prosecuted, 104 (88 percent) were males and 14 (12 percent) were females. One case was unclear. These data confirmed the trend of harassment being a primarily male phenomenon in Negril, although female prostitutes are a visible part of the night-time activities on the streets and in some clubs.

Age

The findings indicated that most of the persons prosecuted were young, within the 21–35 age range, with almost a third (32 percent) in the age group 21–25 (Table 11.5). When compared with official unemployment statistics for the period 1991–1993, there was a correlation between youth unemployment and the number of young people arrested by the police.

Table 11.5   Age of Persons Arrested

Age	Number of Arrests	%
< 21	14	12
21–25	38	32
26–30	28	23
31–35	20	17
36–40	6	5
41–45	3	2.5
> 45	7	6
Not Stated/Unclear	3	2.5
Total	119	100

Source: Compiled from Negril Police data, 1994

The findings further confirmed that although women were more than twice as likely to be unemployed, they were less likely to commit crimes or to be arrested for crimes including harassment (ESSJ 1993a). For example, female adult unemployment for 1992 was 16.3 percent compared to 6.2 percent for males (ESSJ 1992). For 1993, it was 22.4 percent for females compared to 10.9 percent for males. (ESSJ 1993b). This shows that most females in and around Negril were either dependent on males for support or were finding alternative means of income support. These findings indicate the need for further research as well as for special public education and training programmes (targeted at males, in particular, in the 21–35 age group).

The motivation for male harassment appeared to be consistently economic, especially in light of the data emerging from the case studies.

The classification 'labourer' was used to describe an unskilled male available for manual work, and unemployment among this group was high. While not assuming that all unemployed persons were labourers, for purposes of analysis these two categories were combined as they represented persons with very low income or education. The combined data showed that the majority of those arrested (56 percent) were economically marginalized (Table 11.6).

Table 11.6 Occupation of Persons Arrested

Occupation	Number of Arrests	%
Labourer	34	29
Unemployed	32	27
Vendor	5	4
Security Guard	3	3
Water Sports Operator/Instructor	3	3
Other (groups listed below)	42	35
Total	119	101*

* Rounding error

Source: Negril Police data, compiled by Dunn and Dunn (1994)

NOTE: The category 'Other' in Table 11.6 represents many occupational groups. These include accountants, farmers, hairdressers, carpenters, fishermen, hair braiders, ski instructors, dispatchers, painters, carvers, chefs, moneychangers, mechanics, taxi driver/operators, businessmen, salesmen, chauffeurs, and self-employed persons.

Analysis of the police records clearly indicated that more than one-half of those prosecuted were from outside Negril (Table 11.7) . Of this group, over one-half (54 percent) were from communities in Westmoreland such as Sheffield, Grange Hill, Little London, Heritage Road and from Savannah-la-Mar. This profile was consistent with the data from vendors and workers.

Hanover was the second most common parish mentioned, accounting for 31 percent of those arrested. The remaining 18 percent were from overseas, St James, St Elizabeth and St Ann.

The 7 percent with 'no fixed address' could include persons who were homeless or from other parishes.

The review of arrests by the police confirmed that the majority of the persons arrested were unemployed males between 21 and 35 years of age. As previously noted, this suggested that poverty was closely associated with harassment. These persons were more than likely engaged in drug related activities, selling currency, offering services as tour guides, or pimping for prostitutes. The women arrested were sex workers soliciting clients. The most

Table 11.7 Residence of Persons Arrested

Residence (in rank order)	Number Arrested	%
Negril	44	37
Outside Negril (Other Parishes)	64	54
'No Fixed Address'	8	7
Not Stated/ Record Unclear	3	3
Total	119	101*

* Rounding error

Source: Negril Police Data compiled by Dunn and Dunn 1994

common places for harassment were the beaches, the West End Road or private properties. More than one-half of those arrested (54 percent) came from communities outside Negril, mainly from other parts of Westmoreland or Hanover – although a third were from Negril. Most were labourers, with limited education and technical skills. Harassment occurred all during the year with no discernible peak periods. It was also a 24-hour phenomenon, with activities taking place around the clock. This profile was consistent with the data collected from interviews presented in the previous sections.

The Negril police as the main law enforcement agency is faced with the challenging task of keeping the streets safe for both local residents and visitors. Despite the sporadic outbreak of unlawful protests, the fact that visitor numbers to this resort area continue to grow in a generally peaceful context is an indication that the police and law enforcement officers have made a significant difference. Ultimately, however, the solution to the problems of harassment in Negril and elsewhere in the industry is not reached through law enforcement or military means.

CHAPTER 12

Negril

An Analysis of the Data

Analysis of factors contributing to harassment

What are the underlying attitudes and factors that contribute to harassment? The Negril case study provides some answers and indicates the need for further research, as well as a review of policies and programmes to make the industry more sustainable over the next few years. The *Master Plan for Tourism* considers some of these factors but others need to be addressed. The Negril studies showed that harassment has persisted despite the efforts of the police and industry officials to control it. It is perceived to be and is a major problem in Negril. Harassment cuts across all classes, groups and sectors of the industry and is therefore not confined to the micro- businessperson on the streets. Among the common forms identified were:

- Pressuring visitors with unwanted goods and services, some of which are illegal
- Using incentives to entice tourists to patronize a particular business or activity

- Persistently trailing visitors, offering goods and services
- Overcharging for goods and services
- Verbal abuse when services offered are not accepted
- Crime and violence against visitors and tourists

The current studies, given available time and resources, focused mainly on harassment perpetuated by low-income people and did not examine in any detail the activities perpetuated by businesses and persons of a higher socio-economic class. Further research is needed to determine the scope of the problem and the motivations of those persons.

The studies showed that with the exception of touts, there was widespread recognition among all social groups interviewed that harassment is a major deterrent for visitors. The analysis suggested that tackling the root causes rather than the symptoms is a more effective approach. The underlying factors that create the negative attitudes, behaviours and practices associated with harassment must be understood and addressed in order to eradicate the problem. The image emerging from the research is one that portrays tourist harassment as an octopus. Its many tentacles represent various strategies used to ensnare its prey – the tourist. The solutions therefore have to be multifaceted and must address social, economic, political, cultural and psychological concerns.

Not surprisingly, there was a strong correlation between economic poverty and harassment. Jamaica's long experience of structural adjustment programmes, has undoubtedly contributed to a decline in living standards of ordinary people. Protracted negligible economic growth, an undeveloped rural sector; traditional land ownership patterns, the high cost of agricultural inputs and the relatively low returns accruing to small farmers are among the factors that need to be addressed to solve the root causes of harassment.

In addition, globalization and related changes in the external economic and trade environment as well as liberalization of the local market have meant that local farmers have had to compete with cheaper imported agricultural products that are heavily subsidized. These factors have impacted negatively on rural communities creating pressure to find alternatives. In addition, poor social services and underdeveloped rural community life have made migration to urban areas prevalent. It is therefore not surprising that many young people flock to Negril and become involved in activities which are regarded by some as harassment of tourists. Many others (especially males) see these activities as simply attempts to earn a living. Therein lies an opportunity for both public education as well as political and community action to address the underlying issues. In comparison to the challenges and uncertainties of farming, using one's wit to acquire income from visitors is certainly a less stressful and more attractive option for many young people (especially males). But the economic consequences for the industry have to be better explained to these citizens and their support enlisted in less harmful but still productive economic activities.

Unequal development of Negril also emerged as an important factor contributing to harassment. The studies showed that rapid growth without adequate development planning could make tourism unsustainable in the area in the medium to long term. Social, economic, environmental and other forms of development, have to be carefully balanced. Failing this, harassment is likely to continue as a symptom and not a cause of predictable future disinvestment and eventual decline in this resort community.

Related to this is the fact that local people have unequal access to resources from tourism. Unequal growth and development of infrastructure for residents have contributed to this social imbalance. This could lead to a resentment of visitors and a feeling that there are two Negrils and that one should "get something back" from the other. The reality is that while hotels and resort facilities have expanded to meet the growing number of visitors, there has not been comparable expansion of facilities for local people who work in or otherwise contribute to the industry in the area.

The nature of Negril's tourism product may also help to explain harassment. While the industry has undoubtedly been of benefit to many Negril residents, the luxurious type of tourism and the lack of comparable facilities for locals have perpetuated the social and economic inequalities that characterise much of the Jamaican society. This breeds resentment among some sections of society, particularly young unemployed males, whose low levels of education and limited skills make them justify the use of hustling and harassment as their legitimate means to secure their piece of the 'tourism pie'.

Linked to the country's financial problems, economic depression in the surrounding rural parishes also creates pressure on Negril as the sole 'economic oasis' for a large, unskilled population. This raises expectations and demands on visitors and can fuel inclinations towards harassment. The presence of tourists who are perceived to have large disposable incomes provides both motivation and opportunity for people to earn incomes in both the formal and informal sector. Negril has therefore become a 'feeding tree' for parts of western Jamaica. Economic migrants from nearby parishes and the poorer residents who have been unable to find employment in the formal sector are engaged in the 'milking' of this most developed resort area, Negril, as a means of survival.

Vendors, workers and other residents who daily encounter the luxury of tourist facilities may see themselves as coexisting in two radically different social realities. Some also experience conflict, which in turn could contribute to harassment. While further research is needed to explore this relationship in more depth, it must be recognised that where residents of the squatter settlements work in the industry, they do exist in two different worlds. This reality poses a major challenge for creating a service culture within the industry. Their actions and attitudes ultimately have a major impact on the quality of service and on visitor satisfaction.

Lack of diversity in the goods and services offered by local residents to visitors also emerged as a factor contributing to harassment. There is stiff competition between a large number of vendors who sell similar products in the same location to the same group of clients. Their dependence on the industry creates a hustling mentality focused on individual survival. Some vendors may approach visitors to buy goods and services, not realising (or caring) that several other people had already approached them, offering the same things.

The problem of harassment may also be related to newer means of socialisation such as through cable television. Though poor, many local residents now have access to multiple cable and television channels, mostly from the United States. Some of the more popular programmes portray the white and wealthy lifestyles of what we may call here 'Television America'. Images of hard, urban struggle of the ordinary US working family are not frequently portrayed; yet it is these very working people who constitute the majority of visitors to areas such as Negril. Against this background, it is understandable that some local people may automatically link these television lifestyle portrayals with the white North American visitors they see every day. Perceiving that they have money, but without realising how hard many of these visitors have to work to afford a holiday in Negril, touts may feel justified in contriving to separate them from their assumed wealth.

Education and training also emerged as important factors that can reduce harassment. People who are highly educated are less likely to harass visitors in as crude a manner as is often observed on the streets of the resort area. While many in the town have benefited from secondary education at high schools in adjoining parishes, Negril itself has no secondary educational institutions and very few established training facilities. The Negril All-Age School in the centre of the resort engages in important formative education in good attitudes to tourists and tourism. But their efforts are not enough for a town expanding at the rate that Negril is growing. The public sector agency HEART Trust/NTA which provides vocational training for young people, therefore needs to consider establishing a training site in the area to upgrade the level of skills and education of school leavers. Having opportunities for a high school education and a curriculum that builds the knowledge and skills required by the industry, can help to retain more highly educated residents who would normally have to leave the area in order to pursue their educational goals.

The studies also show that linkages need to be established between tourism and other sectors. Evidence that workers entering the sector are marginally more educated and that the staff turnover rate is high suggests that management practices need to be changed to motivate and retain staff in a more educated workforce.

Expanding the microbusiness sector also emerged as a strategy to reduce harassment. Further training of the large number of businesswomen who are vendors needs to be carried out to help them manage and expand their businesses more effectively. This would have a very positive impact on reducing poverty and would help to ensure that they could provide their children with a better quality of life. It was also clear that there were many opportunities to upgrade the skills of workers and vendors to establish small businesses to provide services to both locals and visitors. Investing in the development of specific microbusinesses that are needed would further reduce the pressure on tourism as the dominant means of employment. Training in quality control and product diversification in goods and services would help to reduce harassment. Visitors complained of high prices, but they may be willing to pay higher prices if the quality of products and services are better.

Conclusions and recommendations

Conclusions

The studies concluded that what has been called harassment feeds on economic deprivation, limited education and employment opportunities as well as on poor attitudes that justify taking advantage of others and a 'get-rich-quick' mentality to survive. 'Success' stories of local men and women who have become married to a tourist and migrated have kept hope (and harassment) alive. Despite the many positive comments from local people, the persistence of harassment suggests that there may be an underlying need for 'reverse-exploitation' of wealthy white foreigners who are perceived to have contributed to the economic deprivation of the majority of local people historically, under slavery and colonialism. Rage and resentment cannot therefore be ruled out as contributing factors to aspects of the problem of harassment.

In this context tourist harassment may be equated to a form of rape, in which power is exercised through persistent, sometimes violent pressure, which only eases, when a desired goal is illicitly attained. In the process, the victim or visitor feels violated and the harasser becomes a hunter. Verbal violence and, more rarely, physical attacks sometimes become weapons when services are refused. Physical harassment plays on the emotions of guilt and ignorance. In such more aggressive cases, while public education has a role, the acts of aggression should be considered as crimes that should be prosecuted through the full extent of the law.

Public education, increased police patrols and prosecution, as well as greater vigilance by tourists, through all crucial components, are insufficient as strategies to deal with the problem of harassment. The physical, social and economic infrastructure of Negril must be radically changed. The social gap between locals and visitors must be reduced if the solution is to be effective. Bridging this gap will require an integrated approach in education, training, housing and other amenities required to provide a decent home and community for local residents. Making them equal partners in the tourism industry and sharing the benefits more equitably must also be priorities. The concept of 'Community Tourism' must become an integral part of the product.

According to the *Dictionary of Travel Tourism and Hospitality*, "community tourism requires the involvement of the community and the development of a strong interrelationship between the tourism sector and community members" (quoted in Hayle 2000). The concept is further elaborated by Jayawardena (2001) who discusses it in the retrospective analysis contributed as the final chapter of this book. His conclusions drawn from regional and global perspectives, and those of other researchers cited earlier, coincide with our own findings: local communities must be beneficiaries of the tourist industry and part of the industry's decision making process. Most community members have a vested interest in the success of the industry and would protect it if they feel that they are able to gain access to a fair share of the fruits of Jamaican hospitality.

Recommendations

Positive economic growth at the national level is the only sure way of eradicating the harassment problem. The effective implementation of existing policies and the adoption of new national and area specific programmes must support growth. Among the more important national policy frameworks are the National Industrial Policy, which prioritises tourism as one of the key sectors for growth. The government's Master Plan for Tourism, long in development, while always in need of renewal and revision through consultation with industry players, should not be left to gather dust. Area specific resort boards such as that of the Negril area have established important development plans which are under implementation. These should take more centrally into account the numerous environmental requirements for local industry sustainability. In addition, several studies which have now been done, can provide industry planners and community members with valuable additional insight which can help to make programmes more effective.

Implementation of these policies and programmes will require greater collaboration between key government ministries. Within government, tourism is not just the business of the ministry of tourism and its agencies. The informed inputs of other government departments, private sector interests and international development agencies are also vital for success. Policies, programmes and initiatives will however fail if people in the host communities are not central to the planning.

Spreading the tourism dollar more equitably will also help to change the attitudes and behaviour of many local residents. Diversifying the goods and services available and improving quality and ensuring prices are more competitive and consistent with quality will also help to create a more harmonious climate. Ensuring that the business locations for vendors are attractive, safe, easily accessible to visitors and by actively encouraging them to patronize these locations will also help.

Greater investment in building the human resource capacity in all areas of the industry will also reap considerable dividends while helping to change attitudes and behaviour patterns. Expanding education, training and employment opportunities in Negril and as well as the surrounding parishes are essential for transforming street hustlers and itinerant vendors into real stakeholders.

As James Samuels points out in the Introduction (this volume), management practices and working conditions in the industry must also change to become more consistent with modern management and industrial relations approaches. New strategies have to be developed to manage a more educated workforce.

Create comfort

"When we are comfortable in our homes, we will welcome visitors." So said one of the women interviewed in our fieldwork. Creating this level of comfort will mean re-developing squatter communities, expanding low-income housing, upgrading sewerage and waste disposal systems as well as ensuring that water, roads, electricity, telephones and recreational facilities become basic services to all stakeholders rather than luxuries for a few.

Public education

Changing the external environment is insufficient to promote long-term change. Change must also occur in the attitudes and behaviour of all stakeholder groups. Education and awareness building programmes are therefore vital. Public education programmes must target specific groups of local persons, including vendors, workers, community residents, hoteliers and visitors themselves. Gender must be factored into the equation to recognise that messages that motivate women, may be different from those to which men will respond.

Messages should seek to change the popular perceptions of the tourist, with a focus on making residents see tourists as ordinary people who have saved for a holiday. There should also be a focus on helping vendors recognise that quality, cost, variety and good customer service are keys to success. Messages should link an increase in crime, violence and 'ginnalship' to a reduction in tourist arrivals, resulting in lower earnings for residents. Behaviour patterns that portray good customer service also need to be promoted more widely.

This will complement the training and general thrust in creating a customer service culture.

Public education should also be targeted at visitors, as part of a structured orientation programme prior to or soon after their arrival. Attractive posters and brochures in hotel rooms and guest houses can help to reinforce key messages and help to alert visitors about safe and legal conduct while on holidays. This sort of public education is particularly important for non-English-speaking visitors – in their own language, as the language barrier can make them more vulnerable. Orientation programmes for visitors should include information on the Jamaican currency, the official exchange rate, the proportional value of some common goods and services, advice on tipping and what to do if approached for unwanted goods and services. Their education programme should also, in a 'fun way', equip tourists with tools for survival. Crash courses in bartering, posters and brochures such as 'A Survivor's Guide to Negril', could become an interesting part of marketing the area, while protecting tourists with information to reduce the likelihood of exploitation. Collaboration with environmental education programmes should also be encouraged to improve the general awareness of all groups of the link between environmental protection and the sustainability of tourism.

In their focus group discussions, vendors gave some valuable insights into what could work as public education programmes for the wider local audience. One of the suggestions was to build programmes around the concept of "harassment is . . . " Audio-visuals, drama and small group discussions are also strongly recommended to highlight the range of harassment methods and types of harassers. These should portray the actions and responses of different types of tourists. Among the inputs that could lend popularity to such campaigns would be a competition by local reggae artistes who should be encouraged to perform songs on the issue.

Public education programmes should inform, educate and communicate with different segments of the Negril public. Specific messages aimed at reducing harassment should be communicated through such media as drama, videos, posters, local cable channels, television and national and community radio stations. The key themes emerging from the research are:

- What harassment is
- Harassment hurts tourism
- Most tourists are turned off by harassment
- Harassment robs Jamaicans of dollars and cents

- Treat tourists well as most visitors come on the basis of word of mouth
- Overcharging drives away tourists
- Alternative methods of marketing need to be found
- Provide value for money: most tourists save hard to come for their holiday
- There are different but equally negative forms of harassment
- Tourism is the country's and the community's 'bread and butter' – protect it!
- Every Jamaican can help build tourism – what is your role?
- Put people at the centre of tourism – promote community tourism

Provide training

Several areas for training were identified. Among these were small and micro-business development, management and accounting. Many vendors were vague about the profitability of their business and needed assistance on record-keeping, income and expenditure analysis and marketing. Small business training programmes for vendors should focus on improving quality, cost, marketing, customer service,and pricing, as well as product diversity. Increased diversity and sales are likely to reduce harassment.

Market research to determine what local products tourists are most interested in buying is also needed. There was the perception that many of the current local products had become stale. Some of these should be replaced with new products being introduced periodically. Links with the Edna Manley School of the Visual and Performing Arts, the Creative Production and Training Centre and other relevant institutions would doubtless be an advantage.

Foreign language training also emerged as an area of considerable interest among established vendors. They cited the need to communicate with the large number of non-English-speaking visitors (especially Europeans) who visit Negril. Many come from Germany, Italy and Spain. A seasoned vendor also identified the need for training in English as a foreign language for local people. This vendor noted that several communication problems occurred because foreigners were unable to understand Jamaican English and Creole and many of the Jamaican vendors were unable to express themselves in standard English.

The delivery of cosmetic and personal care services also emerged as another area for training. These included hairdressing. Other services mentioned were vocational training, typing, computer studies, woodwork, sewing, tailoring, painting for art and craft, craft designing, straw craft and cooking. These represented opportunities for alternative employment, which would expand the range of products and services for both locals and visitors. Strengthening links between the tourism sector and the national vocational training programme (HEART Trust /NTA) is also strongly recommended.

Training in life skills such as planning, problem solving, creative thinking and building self-confidence is necessary if the industry and its employees are to face new challenges. These are required in order to change attitudes and behaviour so as to make them more consistent with the requirements of a more globally competitive tourism sector. The needs to improve these skills emerged in discussions with many vendors who wanted to find alternatives, but were unable to focus on their options or identify the skills they would like to learn. This was no doubt a reflection on their education, which limited their perceptions of employment options available locally. A career guidance exposition for local persons should be considered.

Tourism cannot survive without the support and commitment of local people at community and national level. Improving basic infrastructure for residents and ensuring that all stakeholders can contribute to and benefit from tourism is a more sustainable approach to building the industry.

Community Tourism

Applying the Lessons in the Caribbean

CHANDANA JAYAWARDENA*

Communities are inseparably linked to tourism since they enhance and sometimes embody the tourism experience. As the foregoing research studies by Dunn and Dunn demonstrate, in many instances communities are left out of tourism development planning, resulting in resentment and negative actions such as visitor harassment. This brief retrospective analysis discusses community tourism and its implications for holistic sustainable development of the industry. In it we highlight the efforts in countries such as Belize, Dominica and Guyana aimed at developing alternative forms of tourism such as eco-tourism, agro-tourism and community tourism. These approaches address the social resentment sometimes caused from conventional mass tourism and may be seen as alternative scenarios to the approaches critically highlighted in this book.

*Dr Chandana Jayawardena is Senior Lecturer and Academic Director, Msc Programme in Tourism and Hospitality Management, University of the West Indies.

The challenges faced in developing a socially acceptable tourism industry are not limited to the Caribbean region, but also extend to many other parts of the world. Such challenges if addressed, are likely to advance the cause of community involvement, to achieve the ultimate goal of sustainable tourism in the region.

Community

Today when one speaks of 'community' in the context of the tourism sector, often reference is being made in a narrow sense to a rural community located in an area attracting tourists. However, the term 'community' may mean different things to different people. In the context of Caribbean tourism, 'community' may mean any of the following: a group of local people living together in a location attracting tourists; a group of local people living together and sharing common ownership of a tourist attraction (for example, Amerindian peoples in the South American rainforest); or people of a large tourist resort city (for example, people living in Montego Bay, Jamaica).

Tourism related communities can be categorized into four broad segments based on the nature of their involvement in the industry. These are:

- *Communities that have invested in tourism*
  Leading businesspersons as well as small entrepreneurs such as vendors and guesthouse owners are involved in an integrated approach.
- *Communities of workers directly employed in the sector*
  These include hotel employees, airline employees and travel agency employees.
- *Communities indirectly employed/benefiting from tourism*
  These include fishermen supplying hotels, local farmers in tourist areas, domestic employees of a hotel manager and hotel product suppliers (for example, a diver who is employed by a fish supplier to a hotel).
- *Other communities*
  These include all others that are not benefiting from tourism, or communities that are affected negatively by tourism (such as low-income communities bordering on resorts but not involved directly or indirectly in the industry).

As the discussion below of each of these types of community indicates, they can have a major impact for good or ill on tourism in the region.

Communities investing in tourism

In many countries it is claimed that the main reason for local people being excluded from the planning and development of the tourism industry is that they lack the resources (mostly financial) needed to make their input into the industry. Communities, however, possess indigenous knowledge and expertise that are often critical to the sustainable development of the industry. In other instances, they are capable of becoming major stakeholders in the industry through financial investment. Jamaica, for example, has one of the highest ratios of locally owned tourism businesses in the Caribbean. Companies such as the Super Clubs Resorts and Sandals Resorts have become major players in the Jamaican and Caribbean tourism landscapes. Small entrepreneurs are also gaining a foothold in the accommodation sector. Many of the small hotels and guesthouses (often converted family homes) in the Caribbean, like those along the south coast of Barbados, those dotted around St George's basin in Grenada and at Negril in Jamaica are owned by (local) women (Patullo 1996). The high degree of local ownership within the industry contributes to the overall development of the country. While some of these homegrown hotel chains have occasionally been accused of actions which contribute to the degradation of the environment, the success of such companies is sometimes accompanied by a demonstration of social and environmental responsibility and respect for the environment around the resorts. Where such positive actions occur, they enhance the chances of destinations in the Caribbean becoming truly sustainable as sites for tourism development.

Countries such as Belize, Costa Rica, Ecuador and Peru have developed and promoted sustainable tourism since the mid-1980s to generate significant revenue and employment while striving to reduce the negative impacts of the industry (Mitchell 2000). In some countries tourism has evolved to become the mainstay of the local economy where communities are almost totally dependent on tourism and the tourist dollar for their survival. Agriculture and other traditional industries may still exist within these communities but these activities are geared towards satisfying the needs of the tourist market.

In Peru, for example, 'new' forms of community have been encouraged. These ventures have been successful because the country possesses unique historical, cultural and heritage attractions. In Taquile Island in southeastern Peru, tourism development began reluctantly in the 1970s but is now embraced by the community members. The main attraction there is the artisan stores that sell elaborate and sophisticated textiles. According to Mitchell (2000), the form of tourism in this community is significantly controlled in its type, intensity and direction by the Taquileños. Tourism has developed as a major source of income and employment in this community.

Communities of workers directly employed in tourism

Often disguised as simple acts of hospitality, hosting a tourism sector conceals a complicated web of intricate business activities, relationships and negotiations conducted across international borders (Holder 2000). A number of persons find employment in the industry, including in sectors such as travel agencies, airlines, attractions and heritage sites. Some hotel workers have many benefits such as tips, service charges, meals whilst on duty, and in a few cases free accommodation. In general, employees face long and extremely demanding working hours, split shifts and stressful peak periods coupled with the seasonal labour needs. As such, conflicts sometimes occur, resulting in instances of strikes, go-slows, sit-ins and sick-outs that have had a serious impact on the sensitive hotel industry. These are more prevalent in some Caribbean countries than in others. Hotels have used several strategic approaches in dealing with labour situations. Three of the more widely used methods are:

- trying to prevent the formation of a union
- adopting a paternalistic approach
- collaborating with the union (Jayawardena and Crick 2000: 113–28).

Where unions have managed to establish stable employee communities in the hotel sector, particularly in the English-speaking Caribbean, they have managed to negotiate reasonable wages and working conditions. In Antigua, for example, where as early as 1962 agreement had been made with 13 hotels, today, the Antigua Workers' Union (AWU) negotiates with over 100 hotels and guesthouses with most of the island's 6,000 hotel employees represented. Agreements made include clauses on equal pay, maternity leave, redundancy payments, paid vacation leave and sick leave with pay (Patullo 1996). Many hotels are constantly trying to develop incentives and benefits that meet workers' needs and keep them happy. But as is pointed out by some Jamaican workers interviewed in the surveys by Dunn and Dunn, many hotels also fail to meet the financial and other 'job satisfaction' expectations of their employees.

Maintaining a strong community of interest among employees involves giving high levels of motivation. One of the primary factors affecting motivation in the workforce is the relationship between management and workers. The region's institutions and styles of management have been greatly influenced by the colonial plantation structure in which properties were owned by absentee management. Under this model, European owners and local or localised overseers on the one hand, maintained a tense working relationship with enslaved workers and indentured labourers on the other. In this structure, the primary means of increasing production was coercion. Leadership was authoritarian and communication was top down. Unwittingly, many tourism and hospitality companies replicate the old structure by having an expatriate management team that may not be familiar with the customs and value systems of the workers they supervise. All managers, and particularly expatriate ones, therefore, need to be able to understand and respect the customs and habits, values, norms, and attitudes of employees, while demanding the required high standards of performance. As the data from the Negril research study indicate, the future of any form of community tourism will depend on the confidence level, training and cohesiveness of the employees and managers (Dunn and Dunn 1994).

Communities indirectly involved but benefiting from tourism

As a result of the multiplier effect, the benefits from tourism usually filter into many communities. "Beyond the hotels, restaurants and casinos, an unknown amount of 'indirect' employment is generated by the industry, especially in agriculture and handicrafts, transportation, construction and some manufacturing" (Patullo 1996). The benefits to communities are multiplied because of the pervasive and invasive nature of the tourism industry. From airports and seaports to the areas in and around resorts, men, women and children earn money selling craft and other items to tourists. Vending has been an important source of income generation for a large number on people in the formal and informal sectors in the resort areas of Jamaica for many years. Boxill (2000) as well as Dunn and Dunn (1999) indicate that the tourism industry in Jamaica has created a viable market for some persons who are in need of income and who are able to manage their own businesses. In Guyana, some Amerindian communities such as the Santa Aratax Mission of the Pokerero River area earn an income from the manufacture of handicraft, which are sold to both domestic and international tourists who visit the community. Craft items are also sent to the capital city Georgetown where they are sold in gift shops.

The degree of indirect benefit received by communities is related to the level of linkage between tourism and other sectors of the economy. In most agricultural communities, the benefits received from tourism are great since the hotels often depend on these communities to provide produce needed for the guests. In some instances, smaller hotels in the region contribute more to the indirect flow of benefits to these communities. Many of these small establishments depend more readily on local agricultural communities for their food items. They are less likely to import food to be served to their guests. The primary concern when such arrangements exist is the quality of the produce provided to the hotels. In instances where the quality of goods is inadequate, local farmers may need support and technical expertise from the hotel and tourism sector, as well as from the government, to assist in upgrading their standards, increasing the quality of their product and strengthening the network of suppliers.

As a result of this multiplier effect, which generates indirect benefits for local communities, many governments find it difficult to quantify, categorize and capture the 'real' earnings from tourism. Appraisals of the economic benefits from the tourism industry are therefore usually restricted to restaurant earnings and room revenues. In reality some of the true benefits of the industry may have been felt by the person who sells coconut water on the corner, by the farmer who cultivates onions and carrots, as well as by the larger business-person who owns a 200-room hotel.

Other communities

There are a number of regions that depend on the tourism industry for their existence. Invariably, these communities have squatter settlements within or near to them. In Jamaica, for example, squatting around tourism resorts is prevalent. The studies conducted by Dunn and Dunn (1994, 1999) make reference to such communities as Flankers and Canterbury near Montego

Bay. According to Boxill (2000) there is a relationship between perceived economic opportunities and internal migration, as well as between migration and squatting. In most instances, migration is not accompanied by the provision of appropriate housing and other facilities for residents. Poor physical conditions such as overcrowding and congestion, inflated prices, reduced access to beaches and increased pollution may be the norm in many of these areas. While such squatter communities or 'depressed areas' are lacking in adequate social infrastructure, they may be located next to well established tourist resort areas. This contradictory development may result in negative attitudes and practices such as harassment.

Some communities receive little or no direct or indirect benefits from the industry and over time they begin to resent the industry. Despite finding that a large majority of the Jamaican public supports the tourism industry, the data in this study also suggest significant pockets of resentment and even hostility. Holder (2000) perceives a more deep-seated resentment of the industry at every level of (Caribbean) society, a resentment which he argues probably stems from historic sociocultural associations of race, colonialism and slavery. He further states that the people of the Caribbean are forced to choose between an industry that people 'deep down' do not really want, and the economic fruits of that industry which they need and which, it seems more and more, only tourism will provide (quoted by Patullo 1996). To many, tourism in the Caribbean then becomes a 'necessary evil'.

It is important, therefore, to evaluate each community's sensitivity to the industry as a first step in planning sustainable tourism. This is the task to which the authors of this book have set their hands and the results have been instructive as a guide to future planning. The central lesson of this book is that people's involvement and participation in the industry's development should be a constant policy goal.

References

APEC Tourism Working Group. 1998. *The Economic Impact of Travel and Tourism Development*. UK: World Travel and Tourism Council (WTTC).

Boxill, I. 1995. "Crime and sustainable tourism in Jamaica". Kingston: University of the West Indies.

_____. 2000. "Overcoming social problems in the Jamaican tourism industry". In *Turismo en el Caribe/Tourism in the Caribbean*, eds. I. J. Maerk and I. Boxill, 17-40. Mexico: Plaza y Valdez.

Campbell, S., A. Perkins, and P. Mohammed. 1999. "'Come to Jamaica and feel alright': tourism and the sex trade". In *Sun, Sex and Gold: Tourism and Sex Work in the Caribbean*, ed. K. Kempadoo. New York: Rowman and Littlefield Publishers, Inc.

Caribbean Tourism Organisation. 2001. *1999 Statistical Report*. Barbados: Caribbean Tourism Organisation.

Cassell, G., V. George, J. Rao, T. Richards. 2000. "Research for development: strengthening our tourism product". Kingston, University of the West Indies: The Library.

Centre for Population, Community and Social Policy. 1999. "Report on Rapid Assessment of Ocho Rios, St Ann". Mona, University of the West Indies: Department of Sociology & Social Work.

Concise Oxford Dictionary. 1990. New York: Oxford University Press.

Crick, A. 2000. "Personalized service in the small hotel sector: challenges and opportunities". In *Turismo en el Caribe/Tourism in the Caribbean*, eds. I. J. Maerk and I. Boxill, 129–48. Mexico: Plaza y Valdez.

Dunn, L.-D. 1999. *Tourism Attractions: a Critical Analysis of this Subsector in Jamaica*. Kingston: Canoe Press, UWI.

Dunn, L. L. 2000. *Sex for Survival and Status: Rapid Assessment Report on Child Prostitution in Jamaica*. (Prepared for International Labour Organisation). Geneva: ILO/IPEC.

Dunn, H. S., and L. L. Dunn. 1999. "Jamaican attitudes to tourism and to Jamaica Tourist Board Messages". (A report prepared for the Jamaica Tourist Board). Kingston.

Dunn, L. L., and H. S. Dunn. 1994. "Report on visitor harassment and attitudes to tourism and tourists in Negril". Kingston: Jamaica Tourist Board & Tourism Action Plan.

Economist. 1999. *Pocket World in Figures*. London: Profile Books.

Fleischer, A., and D. Felsenstein. 2000. "Support for rural tourism: does it make a difference?" *Annals of Tourism Research* 27(4).

Hayle, C. 2000. "Community tourism in Jamaica". In *Turismo en el Caribe/Tourism in the Caribbean*, eds. I. J. Maerk, and I. Boxill, 165–76. Mexico: Plaza y Valdez.

Hayle, D., and Associates. 2000. *Tourism Master Plan: Carrying Capacity Study*. London: Commonwealth Secretariat.

Holder, J. 1996. "Marketing competitiveness in a new world order: regional solutions to Caribbean tourism sustainability problems". In *Practising Responsible Tourism*, eds. L. C. Harrison and W. Husbands, 145–73. Toronto: Wiley.

_____. 2000. "Island improvement". World Travel & Tourism Development Association Report.

_____. 2001. "Some ideas for tourism change in a changing world". Barbados: Caribbean Tourism Organisation.

Jamaica. Ministry of Health. 1996. "Report of a knowledge, attitude, behaviour and practices study among female commercial sex workers". Kingston: USAID/AIDSCAP / Jamaica Project.

Jamaica. Ministry of Tourism. 2001. *The Ten-year Master Plan for Sustainable Tourism Development*. Kingston: Ministry of Tourism.

Jamaica Hotel and Tourist Association. 1999. "Presentation to National Roundtable Consultation". Kingston, Jamaica (January 27–28).

Jamaica Tourist Board. 1999 and 2000. *Jamaica: Annual Travel Statistics 1999 and 2000*. Kingston: Jamaica Tourist Board.

Jamaican, The. 2000. "The tourism story". *The Jamaican Magazine* (Edition 2000).

Jayawardena, C. 2001. "Tourism and hospitality education and training in the Caribbean: an analysis of recent initiatives". Paper presented at the Pan-American Confederation of Hospitality and Tourism Schools (CONPEHT) Conference, Cuba.

Jayawardena, C., and A. Crick. 2000. "Human resource management in Jamaica: responding to challenging times". In *International Human Resource Management in the Hospitality Industry*, eds. S. M. Hoffman, C. Johnson and M. M. Lefever, 113–28. USA: Educational Institute.

Jayawardena, C., and H. McDavid. 2000. "Implications of agro-tourism in the Caribbean". In *Agro-tourism: a Sustainable Approach to Economic Growth*, ed. P. Collins, 119–35. Trinidad and Tobago: Inter-American Institute for Co-operation in Agriculture.

Jude, G. 2001. "Tourism development in Negril needs more attention". *The Financial Gleaner* (April 6): 4.

Kempadoo K. 1994. "Exotic colonies: Caribbean women in the Dutch sex trade". PhD diss., University of Colorado.

_____. 2001. "Women of color and the global sex trade: transnational feminist perspectives". *Meridians: feminism, race, transnationalism* 1(2): 28–51.

Kempadoo, K., ed. 1999. *Sun, Sex and Gold: Tourism and Sex Work in the Caribbean*. Colorado: Rowman and Littlefield Publishers, Inc.

KPMG/Management Consultants. 1996. *An Agro-Tourism Strategy for Nova Scotia*. Canada: Nova Scotia Agriculture and Marketing.

_____. 2000. *Intra-regional Travel Market Study*. Barbados: Caribbean Tourism Organisation.

McHardy, P. 2001. "Planning for sustainable tourism development". Paper presented at the Second Annual Educators Forum of the Caribbean Tourism Human Resource Council, Antigua.

McIntyre-Pike, D. 1994. "Community tourism encouraged in Jamaica". *The Sunday Gleaner* (February 14): 11A.

Maerk, J., and I. Boxill, eds. 2000. *Turismo en el Caribe/Tourism in the Caribbean*. Mexico: Plaza y Valdez.

Mitchell, R. 2000. "Community tourism in Peru: the island of Taquile, Lake Titicaca". http://www.planeta.com/00/0010peru.html.

Mitchell, R. E., and D. G. Reid. 2000. "Community integration: Island tourism in Peru", *Annals of Tourism Research* 28(1).

Morrison, D. 1999. "Tourism advertising is not where it's at". *The Sunday Observer* (April 11): 8.

"New plan for small hotels". 1999. *The Jamaica Observer* (February 3): 1.

Obermair, K. 1999. *Future Trends in Tourism*. Austria: University of Vienna.

O'Connell Davidson, J. 1996. "Sex tourism in Cuba", *Race and Class* 38: 39–48.

O'Connell Davidson, J., and J. Sanchez Taylor. 1996a. *Child Prostitution and Sex Tourism: Cuba*. Thailand: ECPAT Bangkok.

_____. 1996b. *Child Prostitution and Sex Tourism: the Dominican Republic*.Thailand: ECPAT Bangkok.

Office of the Prime Minister. 1999. *Jamaica's Tourism Industry: a Diagnosis with Strategic Options* (March).

_____. 1999. "Summary of public consultation meetings re Tourism Master Plan (March).

Paris, J., and C. Zona-Paris. 1999. *One Hundred Best All-Inclusive Resorts of the World*. USA: The Globe Pequot Press.

Patullo, P. 1996. *The Last Resorts: the Cost of Tourism in the Caribbean*. UK: Cassell.

Planning Institute of Jamaica. 1992. *The Economic and Social Survey of Jamaica 1992*. Kingston: PIOJ.

_____. 1993. *The Economic and Social Survey of Jamaica 1993*. Kingston: PIOJ.

_____. 1998. *The Economic and Social Survey of Jamaica 1998*. Kingston: PIOJ.

_____. 1999. *The Economic and Social Survey of Jamaica 1999*. Kingston: PIOJ.

_____. 2000. *The Economic and Social Survey of Jamaica 2000*. Kingston: PIOJ.

Sarantakos, S. 1998. *Social Research*. London: Macmillan Press.

Severin, F. O. 2001. "Community development". Paper presented to the students of the MSc. Programme in Tourism and Hospitality Management. University of the West Indies, Mona.

Shaw, S. 2001. "Spring break revenue falls". *The Jamaica Observer* (April 7): 14.

Smith, L. B. 1999. "Flankers: bomb with a short fuse". *The Jamaica Observer* (April 13): 6.

Sproule, K. W. 1995. *Community_based Ecotourism Development: Identifying Partners in the Process*. Wildlife Preservation Trust International.

Statistical Institute of Jamaica. 1998. *Statistical Abstract 1997*. Kingston: STATIN.

Stone, C. 1989. "Report on Tourist Harassment". Kingston.

Tosun, C. 2000. "Limits to community participation in the tourism development process in developing countries". *Tourism Management* 21.

"Tourism under-performing". 1999. *The Sunday Gleaner* (June 6): 3A.

UNDP. 1994. *Human Development Report, United Nations Development Programme*. New York: Oxford University Press.

"Why does Negril draw spring breakers?" 2001. *The Jamaica Gleaner* (April 6): C 1.